Bringing Set and Costume Designs to Fruition

Bringing Set and Costume Designs to Fruition: Made by Teams dives into the collaborative working relationships between set and costume designers and their technical counterparts throughout the theatrical production process, from concept to execution.

Set and costume designers render environments and characters for a wide array of performative events; skilled artisans and technologists bring these visions to life. This book explores the dynamic between those who decide what the set and costumes should look like and those who make them work, including scene designers, costume designers, scene shops, and costume shops. The book discusses how to identify resources, ask the right questions, and engage in healthy collaborations. Following these fundamentals are practical activities and interviews with industry professional that demonstrate how these skills can be applied to a broad range of productions and other avenues for creative design and production.

Bringing Set and Costume Designs to Fruition is written for emerging professionals in set and costume design, as well as students in courses across a theatre degree program, including stagecraft, costume construction, scene design, and introduction to theatrical design and production.

Jennifer Dasher (she/her) is an Assistant Professor of Costume Design in the College of the Arts at The University of Florida and the recipient of the Morris Foundation Visiting Artist Grant at the University at Buffalo. Jen was recently selected as a TEDx speaker, amplifying the intersection of visual messaging, design, and identity in "Why is Anyone Listening to Me?". She is the owner of J.Dasher Creative, a creative studio that has produced designs for Cirque du

Soleil, Paula Abdul, Glimmerglass Opera, The Washington Ballet, Ford's Theatre, PBS, Ballet X, and a selection of Broadway and Off-Broadway works. Jennifer received her BFA from Texas Christian University and MFA from The University of Arizona.

Lynne M. Koscielniak (she/her) is a member of United Scenic Artists Local 829 in the set and lighting design categories, and a Professor of Theatre in the Department of Theatre and Dance at the University at Buffalo. Lynne's work has been seen both regionally and internationally, including at the Prague Quadrennial of Performance Design and Space and at World Stage Design Expositions. Select honors include an emerging designer residency at the Steppenwolf Theatre Company, the Michael Merritt Scholarship for Excellence in Design and Collaboration, and a Kennedy Center American College Theatre Festival Gold Medallion Award for extraordinary contributions to the teaching/producing of theatre. Lynne received her BA from Buffalo State College, SUNY and holds an MFA in Stage Design from Northwestern University.

Jonathan Shimon (he/him) is an Associate Professor of Theatre Technology in the Department of Theatre and Dance at the University at Buffalo and an Associate Trainer for The Chicago Flyhouse. His specialties include industrial hygiene for theatre, scenic automation, structural design and analysis, rigging, material labor estimation, and management. A certified theatrical rigger and recognized trainer through the Entertainment Technician Certification Program, Jon was selected to be the Technical Director for the US entries in the 2019 Prague Quadrennial of Performance Design and Space. Jon received his MFA in Technical Production from Florida State University.

Bringing Set and Costume Designs to Fruition

Made by Teams

Jennifer Dasher
Lynne M. Koscielniak
Jonathan Shimon

NEW YORK AND LONDON

Designed cover images: Top: © Paul Calandra, Director of Photography, University at Buffalo Center for the Arts
Bottom: © Artpark & Company, Lewiston, NY

First published 2023
by Routledge
605 Third Avenue, New York, NY 10158

and by Routledge
4 Park Square, Milton Park, Abingdon, Oxon, OX14 4RN

Routledge is an imprint of the Taylor & Francis Group, an informa business

© 2023 Jennifer Dasher, Lynne M. Koscielniak, and Jonathan Shimon

The right of Jennifer Dasher, Lynne M. Koscielniak, and Jonathan Shimon to be identified as authors of this work has been asserted in accordance with sections 77 and 78 of the Copyright, Designs and Patents Act 1988.

All rights reserved. No part of this book may be reprinted or reproduced or utilised in any form or by any electronic, mechanical, or other means, now known or hereafter invented, including photocopying and recording, or in any information storage or retrieval system, without permission in writing from the publishers.

Trademark notice: Product or corporate names may be trademarks or registered trademarks, and are used only for identification and explanation without intent to infringe.

Library of Congress Cataloging-in-Publication Data
Names: Dasher, Jennifer, author. | Koscielniak, Lynne M., author. | Shimon, Jonathan (Professor of theatre technology), author.
Title: Bringing set and costume designs to fruition : made by teams / Jennifer Dasher, Lynne M. Koscielniak, Jonathan Shimon.
Description: New York, NY : Routledge, 2023. | Includes index.
Identifiers: LCCN 2022054702 (print) | LCCN 2022054703 (ebook) | ISBN 9781032108414 (hardback) | ISBN 9781032108384 (paperback) | ISBN 9781003217329 (ebook)
Subjects: LCSH: Theaters—Stage-setting and scenery. | Costume design. | Teams in the workplace. | Theater—Production and direction.
Classification: LCC PN2091.S8 D285 2023 (print) | LCC PN2091.S8 (ebook) | DDC 792.02/5—dc23/eng/20230313
LC record available at https://lccn.loc.gov/2022054702
LC ebook record available at https://lccn.loc.gov/2022054703

ISBN: 978-1-032-10841-4 (hbk)
ISBN: 978-1-032-10838-4 (pbk)
ISBN: 978-1-003-21732-9 (ebk)

DOI: 10.4324/9781003217329

Typeset in Palatino
by codeMantra

Contents

Acknowledgements vii

1 Introduction 1

2 Me Team 18

3 Self-managed Team 54

4 Functional Team 81

5 Contract Team 109

6 Pivoting Teams 143

7 Conclusion 178

Index 183

Acknowledgements

We would like to recognize all of the teams we have been a part of; without these collaborations this book would not have come to fruition. We acknowledge Kambrea Lagrosa, Research Assistant, and give thanks to the professionals who contributed to our industry perspectives throughout the book.

1

Introduction

READING THIS BOOK

Bringing Sets and Costumes to Fruition: Made by Teams builds upon foundational training and experience in scenic and costume programs and environments. No two production environments are identical, but the skills needed to successfully engage in the collaborative processes resulting in effective visual storytelling are the same. The text broadly defines the team as designer and technician, for theatre or an adjacent field. There are teammates mentioned that are on the broader production team, but the focus of this book is on design and technical collaboration. Within that broad definition of team, team structures are broken down and defined as:

Me Team: one practitioner (designer/technician) who is responsible for the design and fabrication/procurement of scenic or costume elements.

Self-managed Team: two practitioners, a designer and a technician, who divide tasks from design through fabrication/procurement of scenic or costume elements.

Functional Team: a fleshed-out team comprised of specialists who will address various tasks required to design and fabricate/procure the scenic or costume elements.

Contract Team: professional businesses, each contracted to provide a portion of the services, required to design and fabricate/procure the scenic or costume elements.

Pivot Team: a team that utilizes the skills of a design or technical theatre practitioner in making work outside of the "norm" of live performance on a stage.

The team structures addressed in this book are not inclusive of every structure within live entertainment. What applies to one team structure can easily be translated into another team structure as the need or opportunity arises. For our purposes, each team structure has a chapter to itself, where an analysis of the resources and processes typical for the scale of production the team often operates is presented. Industry perspectives and practical activities further define and contextualize the collaborative dynamics and team structures discussed. The text leads with the soft and hard skills that allow for healthy design and technical collaborations to exist, and consistently addresses the pre-production and actualization phases of theatre production, as well as the "run of show" considerations throughout.

FUNDAMENTAL COLLABORATIVE SKILLS

Positive production processes are a result of individuals having a solid understanding of how their contribution relates to the total outcome, while being able to hold their own in specific areas of expertise. To achieve this, designers and technicians rely on a solid combination of soft and hard skills.

Combining soft and hard skills leads to tangible results such as the design package, technical paperwork, well-maintained work space, and the production itself. These outcomes directly correspond to the three phases of making described in the book: pre-production, actualization, and the run.

Soft skills are most often interpersonal, undervalued, and untaught. These skills are vital to the success of the team and developing or practicing one skill is often contingent upon practicing the others. Without a foundation and practice that utilizes these soft skills, collaboration is fraught. The more members of the team are well-versed in fundamental skills for collaboration the smoother the process will be. Similarly, when one team member is unskilled in these fundamentals, skilled practitioners can draw upon their depth of soft skills to meet the moment without contributing to the stressful process.

Set and costume practitioners also possess a series of hard skills that are comparable. They imagine, fabricate, engineer, and repurpose tactile elements that are inhabited by actors to convey information relating to the story being presented. Hard skills are discussed in terms of hat-wearing. What hat one wears during a production process varies based on the creative objective and the resources available. Acknowledging what "hats" you are wearing is essential to the health of the collaboration. Each hat assumes a level of competency with hard skills that form the foundation of most training programs and apprenticeships.

Soft and hard skills thought of in terms of "DIRECT ACTION" will lead to positive production outcomes.

The **DIRECT** soft skills that enable someone to be a good team player include:

- Dependability
- Interpersonal communication
- Respect
- Emotional intelligence
- Critical thinking
- Transparency

The **ACTION** hard skills that lead to tangible deliverables include:

- Analytic ability
- Creative techniques
- Transformational processes
- Investigatory research
- Operational skills
- Negotiation tactics

Soft skills

Dependability
Dependability is the ability to be relied on. It is a quality that is interwoven into the practice of all who successfully engage in live entertainment as a career. Dependable collaborators develop a rapport with teammates because they can be trusted to plan, communicate, and work productively towards collective deadlines. Dependability results in excellent planning, priority setting and execution. Workflows are efficient and processes are clear. Communication with all stakeholders is important and dependable. Collaborators make every effort to follow through and meet commitments. When

a commitment cannot be kept, this is communicated early, and adjustments are made with the team. Communicating early keeps chaos to a minimum which is a welcome result respected by all collaborators. The positive impact dependable collaborators have on the process and teammates makes them valuable teammates likely to be hired again.

Interpersonal Communication

Interpersonal communication is the exchange of information to achieve better understanding. A vital skill for successful collaboration, interpersonal communication allows relationships to function; without functioning relationships collaboration cannot happen. In collaborative production environments, there are two types of communication skills that should be honed: visual and verbal. Interpersonal communication is often thought of as the expression of one's ideas and taught as "how can I better express myself?" But, in collaborative environments, successful dissemination and reception of information is fundamental. Active listening is the counterpart to expressing oneself as it allows teammates to express themselves and be heard. Active listening is listening to understand versus listening to respond and should be practiced both in moments of visual communication and verbal communication. Active looking while visually communicating prevents unnecessary questioning, as ideas are often clarified in a well-thought-out visual mechanism for communication. When we actively listen, we listen to understand and our minds are clear and open to the ideas being presented. Conversely if we are listening to respond, our minds are focused on the response causing us to miss things as collaborators. Taking a moment to take in an idea as both technicians and designers feeds a fruitful conversation and builds relationships with our team.

Respect

Respect is found in innumerable forms, respect for one's self, respect for the work, respect for another, respect for time, respect for boundaries, and so on. The foundation of successful teams is the fundamental respect that your team members each contribute to the project in a valuable way. From artistic directors to shop assistants everyone on a team contributes, every job is important. Respect yourself, ask for what you need to do your job to the best of your ability with the skills and resources that you have. Words matter, what you say may have an impact on those around you in ways you did not intend or foresee. The best days in live events are when a team accomplishes the seemingly impossible without conflict. Treating people nicely and being appreciative of their work can go very far, treat others how you want to be treated. Saying "thank you" is free. Production objectives may shift as discoveries are made in a rehearsal process. In order to respect time and boundaries, reserve time for the unexpected. This is especially critical in situations where it's unlikely additional funding will be made available.

Emotional Intelligence

Emotional intelligence is commonly thought of as the ability to perceive, use, understand and manage emotions. Collaborative environments are most successful when two components of emotional intelligence are present: self-awareness and empathy. Self-awareness means you know your own emotions, motivations, and blind spots, while being aware of how they impact the team and/or work. Empathy is putting yourself emotionally or cognitively in another's shoes. The ability to shift between the two encourages relational bonding. Checking in with ourselves throughout collaborative processes, becoming aware when emotions rise, being able to pause and manage those emotions diffuses conflict. Allowing ourselves to take the perspective of our collaborator increases outcomes and reduces stress on the team. Design and production teams create work that serves stories. When individuals frame our artistic objective for the set or costumes as "the idea" rather than "my idea" we acknowledge the equitable contributions to the collaboration and confirm that this isn't personal. Within collaborative exchange this helps individual contributors remember they are not being critiqued, the idea is being assessed through a design approach and feasibility lens.

Critical Thinking

Critical thinking is the analysis and evaluation of an issue to form a judgment. It is a skill that is most immediately thought of as tangible problem-solving which is easily visible in design and production environments. Problem-solving of this nature typically relies on parameters and the practice of the craft to create a solution. Critical thinking in collaborative teams is a complex combination of steps that results in decision-making. It is self-directed, self-disciplined, self-monitored, and self-corrective thinking that utilizes skills including observation, analysis, interpretation, reflection, evaluation, inference, explanation, problem-solving, and decision-making. Critical thinking presupposes rigorous standards and a commitment to overcoming egocentrism. Decisions are not rendered simply because an individual wants them to be. A set of data is observed, analyzed, and evaluated to become the basis of the decision often overriding the individual.

Transparency

Transparency is the act of telling the truth even when no one asks for it. Successful teams trust one another. A key to building trust is transparency. By creating a habit of open reasoning and decision-making you create an environment where no one questions your motivations. Transparency for artists can be challenging as exposing in-process work can feel unnecessarily vulnerable. But sharing your discoveries throughout the process brings the team further into the world you are co-creating. Sharing concerns and/or blocks allows the team to be actively participating in your collaborative process which is ideal in storytelling. Collaborative teams are not merely about checking in and making sure the scenic designer and costume designer do not choose the same palette, but the entire world of the story is built brick by brick to seamlessly invite the audience into the experience. Transparency can be implemented in every part of the production process from the theoretical and inspirational to the materiality and feasibility.

Hard Skills

Analytic Ability
Designers and technicians alike, in order to be informed collaborators, use analytic ability to understand the givens of their production, from source material to venue. This is necessary in order to identify the creative and technical problems that need to be solved by the teams who are charged with visually assisting the audience

to gain a full understanding of the story being told, while creating an environment and costumes that function to enhance the actor's ability to tell the story. All team members benefit from text analysis, so that their contributions respond to the needs of a particular play or musical book and score, and their problem-solving is geared towards a particular title, not theatre practice in general. All team members benefit from a thorough diagnostic of what the venue provides, with an eye towards audience–performer relationship, stage machinery and physical space available, and safety requirements for the jurisdiction. Analytical ability is required to develop concept statements and feasibility studies for productions.

Creative Techniques

Set and costume team members require experience in creative techniques used for visual communication and should be well practiced in applying the elements and principles of design to their stage designs. Manual and digital techniques for visual communication are honed and include but are not limited to: drafting, drawing, engineering, modeling, and rendering. Ideas need to be put on paper or worked out on screens so that team members who propose what things look like can have a constructive back and forth with those that will provide technical direction or costume direction to bring the work to fruition. Likewise, technical and costume directors need to explain to the "shop-oriented" team members any and all engineering they have devised to execute the designs. Creative techniques are used in the pre-production process to assemble a design package as well as a technical packet.

Transformational Processes

What is proposed in the design package, and illustrated in a technical packet, is realized in full scale through transformational processes. Wood, steel, foam, hardware, and paint, as examples, combine to make scenic units that evoke a particular place. Fabric is draped on bodies, bought clothes are modified to appear of another time, items are dyed to the right hue. Any and all techniques that relate to the manipulation and modification of materials that result in the manifestation and fabrication of the sets and costumes themselves, fall under transformational processes.

Low-tech and high-tech solutions are used to transform materials. From woodworking and stitching, to artisan work such as scene painting, soft sculpture, and foam carving, set and costume team members are experts at using their tech theatre basics to transform ordinary objects into the extraordinary. Expertise in time-honored fabrication processes and ability to integrate machine building are equally valued – the key is choosing the appropriate process for the scenario, and that is where the expert skill lies.

Investigatory Research

Dramatic works can be set in any time, place, season, and cultural context. Set and costume practitioners need to immerse themselves in the character's world, often described as "world of the play." Connotative research, that allows designers to emotionally connect to the world of the play, is useful as art images that represent the tone of the work, or connect to a theme, can inspire visual solutions. Denotative research that provides insight into the architecture and style lines of the time the play is set is invaluable. Factual research is just as integral to generating the concept as it is to executing the design. Technicians research the best tools and techniques for the job, investigate the suitability and availability of materials, and test the durability of the goods produced. Investigatory research requires strong library skills, the willingness to conduct primary research when necessary, and knowledge of how to cite one's resources.

Operational Skills

As a member of a set and costume team, you will control systems and machines that move a design through the pre-production phase, to the actualization phase (including build and technical rehearsals), to the run. Computer skills are a must, encompassing professional email composition, spreadsheet creation, use of specialty software for computer aided design, cloud collaboration, calendar management, and web portfolios. The list of tools that can be used to work with hard and soft materials to make sets, props, and costumes is endless. Set and costume practitioners may be experts at a short list of tools and/or may have experience with a broad assortment of tools for fabrication/modification. To name a few: table saw, drill press, sewing machine, and serger; as well as hand tools such as screw guns, needle, and threads. Processes such as rigging, automated control, draping and tailoring imply high-level operational skills. Stage machinery from fly systems, to slip decks, to traps must be operated by experts with strength in safe work practices. It is the same for processes that involve chemicals and/or heat such as use of industrial washers, steamers, dye vats, and welding equipment. Expert knowledge of tool usage is required to make the plans and to make the actual items. Set and costume practitioners possess the ability to work "in scale" as well as in full scale, so the type of tools they are able to operate can have significant breath, especially if they work on a variety of team structures.

Negotiation Tactics

Design concepts are finalized through negotiation. In each and every instance of set and costumes coming to fruition, time, money, and resources are factors that inform what may be accomplished for opening night. The act of negotiation between all stakeholders within the set or costume team, and across all the teams contributing to a single production, becomes fraught when even a single party insists on there being one right answer to a creative problem or solution. Stating the problem, such as there needs to be a sittable or we need to represent a royal figure, allows for more than one right answer for this production, this time, with these parameters. Maybe this time we have the time, money, and resources to build the throne if we decide to rent the costume or modify stock, or perhaps if we use a cube from stock as the sittable, the royal costume could be built from head to toe. Independent team meetings as well as production meetings are important so that the big picture is kept at the forefront of all decision- making.

Negotiation tactics are closely tied to the idea of feasibility. Feasibility in terms of contract – is the monetary and/or experiential compensation enough for taking the work in the first place to be feasible in terms of making a living? Feasibility in terms of budget – does the production organization have realistic aspirations for the scope of production given the material budget provided? If not, can the team clarify and discuss monetary resources versus expectations before they begin the work? Feasibility in terms of schedule – are the hours the set or costume team afforded in the work rooms and on stage adequate for what is trying to be achieved? If not, take an opportunity to discuss that before you even begin. And, things don't always go as planned, so budgets and schedules may indeed be an ongoing point of negotiation, although a good faith effort should be made to stay within the guidelines provided at time of contract.

Throughout the book, the idea of feasibility is introduced in relation to the distinct set and costume team structures. The set and costume activities in the book draw attention to the same production challenge, a hardwood floor treatment and a three-piece suit, and suggest questions that surround "the making" of these elements to illustrate how feasibility questions can be tailored to the size of the team. All of these activities stem from the core ideas illustrated in the feasibility flowchart.

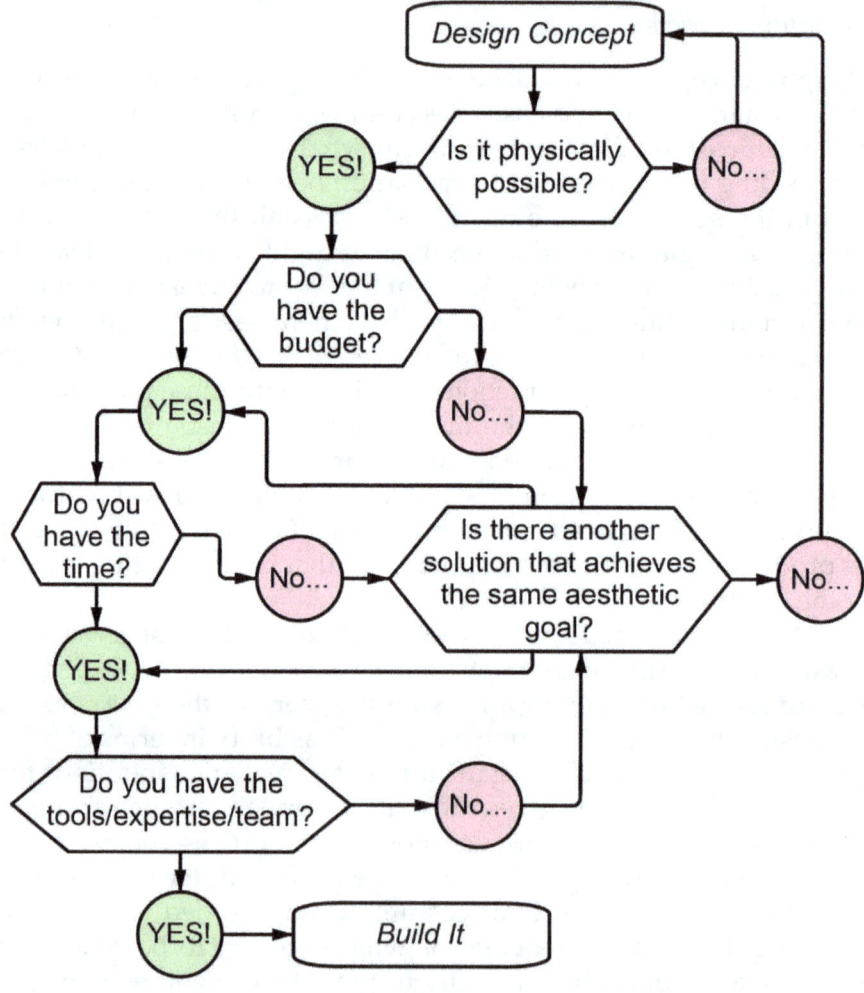

FIGURE 1.1 Feasibility Flowchart.

METHODS OF DESIGN AND PRODUCTION PROCESS

Collaborative teams will vary based on several factors related to the producing organization and the project. In the subsequent chapters we will discuss best practices for collaboration through a lens that changes with the structure of the team and the scale of the production. In order to do so, it is important to have a foundational understanding of the process designers and technicians undertake from page to stage. There are three phases to this process: pre-production, actualization, and the run. As a foundation, this process is described as a linear process. However, it should be noted in practice that the process can flow from one step to another and back again depending on the work being produced.

At the conclusion of each chapter there is an activity that set and costume practitioners alike can use as a point of reflection or as a group-think exercise for their production team, meant to enhance collaborative artmaking. These exercises are meant to inspire conversations around the process of making as a collective, a process where space is made for practitioners to contribute and share expertise in an effort to lift ideas up, rather than push a separate agenda. These activities are an invitation for set and costume practitioners to pause before they jump in and tackle the dramatic work at hand. These conversations are rare in theatre production processes, as set and costume teams are assembled, and go straight to meeting the deadlines, but it is in these conversations that we may determine how we cooperate and when we collaborate. An example of cooperation is when a designer formats a technical draft in the scale a technician prefers, where a collaboration is when the design and technical expert carve the time to work together to accomplish a solution that meets the aesthetic need and the structural requirements of a scenic or costume element.

PROCESS: PRE-PRODUCTION

Pre-production begins once contracted and moves through the drawing and rendering phase. It is the embarkation by the team in a collaborative process. The design is therefore not separate from the realization; and successful realization is based on structures and resources. Broad questions to ask at contracting to determine structures and resources for a project include:

- What is the size and structure of the team?
- Who is on the team and when does their contract begin?
- How does this project fit into the organization's season and does the organization have specific goals for the project?
- What is the materials budget and what does that cover?
- How does the producing organization define your position?

With the information gathered by asking these questions, design and production teams can move forward.

Dissecting the Source Material

Design teams utilize source material (text, movement, music, etc.) to create visual concepts and language to tell a story in a live environment. Most designers are in the habit of engaging with source material multiple times to gather cues, emotionally connect, and look for specificity. Questions to ask:

- What is this story about?
- What images stand out?
- How does it feel?
- What is the location and the time?
- Is there a particular prop, action, or garment called out that will inform the design?
- Are there special effects that will require creativity and resource allocation to achieve?
- Are there consumable items?
- What are the given circumstances of the venue?

Developing a Point of View as a Team

The team's collective point of view will be the lens through which the visual world is established. It is less common in theatrical structures for directors to be the vision and designers to work within that vision than in the theatre of the past. In professional practice, the vision (or concept) for the piece emerges from the collaborative work between directors, dramaturgs, and design teams. In order to fully engage in developing a vision, designers must understand their own point of view and actively listen to other points of view. While dissecting the source material, designers will naturally respond emotionally to the piece. Refining these emotions and expressing them visually will help the individual both understand their point of view and express that point of view to the team. Questions to ask:

- What is important to me about this work?
- What do I want the audience to experience?
- What is important to my collaborators about this work?
- What do my collaborators want the audience to experience?
- What was the playwright's intent?

Establishing Priorities

Priorities can be determined in three general ways: story-driven, circumstance-driven, and concept-driven.

Story-driven priorities will have emerged through the dissection of the source material. At minimum, design and fabrication must address the needs of the script. Lay out these needs with the director before concept discussions so that script requirements are part of the conceptual discussion and not an after-thought. When navigating resources, the needs of the script must be met or adjustments to the script must be determined by the director.

Every production has given circumstances that drive design and production priorities. Given circumstances can be intrinsic to the space: a lack of offstage space, a quick load-in/load-out process. They can be dictated by the type of production: musicals require more from scenic and costume departments alike: stage space must consider orchestra needs, scenic construction must accommodate dancing and potentially noisy movement, shoes must be selected carefully for the comfort of the dancer and take into consideration the treatment on the floor, costume shapes and fit must accentuate the movement intrinsic to the choreographic style. Finally, given circumstances can be determined by casting choices. While one might argue this is not a "given," design teams have no control (nor should they) over the casting. As we move into more inclusivity it is imperative that design teams see casting as a given circumstance that guides creativity rather than a challenge that needs to be overcome. Costume departments are most impacted by casting choice which can profoundly change the way a designer and audience views a character. Placing value on each character and designing for a variety of shapes, sizes, and ethnicities promotes creativity and encourages more complex character and design choice. Because of heightened creativity, characters who might not otherwise can become the priority for resources.

Concept-driven priorities become evident as the design team works with the director to establish a point of view. The point of view a production will take impacts the choices each designer makes and guides how they prioritize resources moving forward. Questions to ask:

- What is essential to include in my design to express the point of view of the team?
- Is there balance between each area's design that expresses the point of view of the team?

Determining the Design Approach

The design approach finds a balance between priorities, the point of view, and production parameters. In the subsequent chapters we will discuss best practices for working within production scope as defined by type of collaborative team. Designers cannot effectively determine design approaches without engaging in collaboration with technicians. A proper assessment by both technician and designer sets the team up for a successful and productive actualization process.

The design package and technical packet are two tangibles from the pre-production process. In general terms, the design package will include a concept statement, research boards, a visual presentation of the concrete design idea through sketch, model, rendering or collage, and technical information via drafting, costume plots, paint elevations, swatches, and lists. A technical packet may include itemized budgets, build calendars, build drawings, photos of items to be incorporated, and procurement information.

PROCESS: ACTUALIZATION

Once a design team has worked with both director and technician to establish a design approach and complete the design process, actualization begins. Actualization is the period during which designers and technicians will closely collaborate to bring the design to life. A technician's art requires analysis of a designer's work and transition from the theoretical to the tangible. Engagement between designer and technician should be very fluid where each understands and tends to their own role while remaining communicative and responsive with the team. Designers have the added collaborative work of continuing to engage the director and performers in what is being realized. Bringing directors, other members of the design team, and performers into the production process at key points can prevent a large volume of revisions during the tech process.

Lead technicians have the added collaborative work of engaging fellow technicians and artisans in the processes by which elements will be modified, fabricated or otherwise prepared.

Revisions are built into the theatrical process. As directors and performers work to create the physicality of the performance there will be discoveries along the way that will undoubtedly require design revisions. Although design and production teams typically begin well in advance of rehearsal processes, flexibility and openness to the process that unfolds in rehearsals is essential to successful collaboration. The actors are co-creators of the story with the directing, design, and production teams. Throughout the rehearsal process, actors discover the story and build characters. This discovery can include needs that must be addressed by the design and production departments. Character creation is most impactful on costume design and production teams but can also impact props and scenic designers. The action of the performer must be safely accommodated by set components. Engagement throughout the rehearsal process both through formal meetings and informal attendance of rehearsal illuminates the direction the production is headed and enables designers and technicians to flag any shifts that impact their department. This engagement also allows departments to shift the direction of choices being made in the rehearsal process that are not able to be safely and effectively accommodated.

While allowing for revisions is essential to the process, equally as important is determining the feasibility of revisions. Feasibility can be related to budget of time, available personnel, or the complexity of a request. To balance the ability to respond to revisions that are emerging from rehearsals, design and production teams should allocate a contingency during preproduction. Contingency should equate to both budget and labor. A simple way to determine contingency is through a percentage of money and time held back. Time ought to be held by designers and technicians alike through the entire tech process to accommodate revisions.

PROCESS: THE RUN

The run of the show changes the dynamics of a team. While each team member is still invested in the success of opening night and subsequent performances, designers move into a passive role while technicians take the lead. Technicians in the shop may be called upon to help maintain the integrity of the work; this occurs on a sliding scale depending on the needs of a production and the size of the wardrobe team. Additionally, the performer has a more substantial role on your team. The goal during the run is to maintain the integrity of the design including its function. Not only does this honor the work of design and production teams but it creates consistency for performers as well. Maintenance needs will arise unpredictably and should be attended to, which will achieve consistency and result in a great run.

The conclusion of a run is a bittersweet moment for most collaborators on most productions. A sense of accomplishment and closing of the work is always fulfilling to theatre artists. Individual roles during the strike process will be addressed in subsequent chapters but continued rooting of oneself in the fundamental collaborative skills and remembering that you are a part of a team will result in a more fulfilling strike process.

IN SUMMATION

Bringing Set and Costume Designs to Fruition: Made by Teams focuses on the work that is required to bring set and costume design to fruition, and asserts that set and costume practitioners who work on horizontal team structures maximize outcomes, versus those that work in hierarchical structures. By exploring the hats that set and costume practitioners wear in different production scenarios, we emphasize the broad range of skills that individuals bring to a process and reinforce how a good understanding of the team member strengths can make way for the best possible end results. We aim to create a dialogue around the possible work environments theatrical designers and technicians can thrive in, empowering emerging and seasoned practitioners to position themselves on teams in capacities that satisfy their interests and put their strengths to good use. We call attention to the need for sustainable practices in the making of sets and costumes at all levels of production. Too often the presence of set and costume shops, or the persons that represent these rooms, can give the illusion that the organization has the means to produce sets and costumes the likes of which one might see at a large regional theatre, when in actuality their staff structures may be that of a small company. When team size is acknowledged, organizations can look at the scale and scope of production through a lens that fits their company or program, and set expectations that maintain a level of sustainability for experts and emerging professionals alike.

2
Me Team

For the set or costume practitioner who works at such a scale that a discipline-specific team is required to meet all design objectives, the idea of the "me" remains relevant. Individual accountability transcends the idea of solo work, and can serve as a reminder to individuals to be clear on what their responsibilities are within the context of a larger working group, and in light of the creative objectives at hand.

DEFINITION

Who is a "me?" We have found ourselves working on projects where the production team includes one specialist from each of the disciplines (sets, costumes, lights, sound, etc.) we generally expect to be involved when making a play. These specialists are responsible for any and all concepts related to their discipline, and also responsible for realizing the concepts for the performance itself. We have also found ourselves in discipline-specific teams, where multiple people direct their expertise to certain production tasks within the discipline. In these instances, we must reflect on the role of the individual, the "me," and decide who will take ownership of certain aspects of the decision-making, as well as who will ultimately accomplish what tasks related to producing the work. The play presents one set of givens, an individual's capabilities and resources present another. This chapter invites you to pause, reflect, and take stock of what you can bring to the table so that ambition doesn't control the making at the expense of mind, body, and pocketbook.

The me team can be found within many levels of producing structures but is most commonly found where resources are limited or the needs of a production small. One example would be a one-person show requiring little to no scenery. Me teams also work on larger-scale productions with limited staffing resources within an organization. Because the me team requires no in-department collaboration, workflow is determined by the solo practitioner and completed by that same practitioner, making self-awareness the key to success.

FORM AND FUNCTION

The me team in a theatrical context is possible within a "collaborative," where interdisciplinary artists unite to make a singular work. A "me" generally has a broader scope to their expertise. The "me" may be a technician who takes the director's needs and wants for a scenic environment or costumes at large, and makes them happen – perhaps many steps in the pre-production phase are skipped. A napkin sketch becomes a box set as one person pulls walls from the warehouse, a page of research becomes the guide to pull applicable garments from stock. The "me" might be a designer who has the time and energy to move their idea from concept to reality, and finds satisfaction in wearing several hats. They may be an expert maker, or a hobbyist helping the local company. A specialist is not autonomous, they have a different kind of team dynamics, a diverse team that shares the ability to analyze text and tell stories, but comes to the project with distinct making abilities. In looking at the me team, we are able to acknowledge the pressures and challenges that are inherent in this kind of work, and have offered strategies for realizing designs in these scenarios.

This investigation of the me team looks at the solo set and costume practitioner in instances where they function as their own "shop" in the context of collaborative theatre making. It also examines the role of the me, defined as an individual set/costume practitioner on a set/costume team, with an eye towards best practices for taking responsibility and meeting deadlines to best serve the team and the production objectives as a whole.

For our purposes, we assume the theatrical work at hand is live or recorded in front of a live audience for streaming. We create an environment for the event, characters costumed for the occasion inhabit the space, directors and choreographers work with performers to fill the space with movement, voice and intentions. Technology infuses the performance – from Foley sound to digital music, from single lamps to elaborate rigs of lighting fixtures, from projected still images to film on screens, any and all tools of artistic expression that serve the story are fair game for the collaborative. The script or story outline from an artistic director or ensemble informs the nature of the interdisciplinary team required to make the work. An interdisciplinary production team might include me teams with broad titles such as movement coordination, set production, costume production, digital effect lead, and audio specialist. This way of working can be exhilarating as the individual designer/technician gets in the trench with the other departments, and works to envision and realize the work from start to finish. A level of personal touch on all items in a team member's discipline can be very fulfilling to some theatre artists.

Solo practitioners bring resources beyond skills to the me team. In lieu of a shop space outfitted with equipment, solo practitioners may need to utilize what they have in their own kit. The producing organization will make an assumption that any design work proposed will be possible both within materials budgets and utilizing tools the practitioner already possesses. In this way, practitioners can find themselves in challenging situations if designing to a scale or complexity that they themselves cannot realize. Challenging oneself to realize some element of design that is slightly beyond the skillset currently possessed can be thrilling but the practitioner should keep this to scale. One challenge may illuminate the design as well as ignite learning and passion, but an entirely out of the box design that is a challenge to realize on multiple levels will lead to an unfulfilling, stressful collaboration. The me team becomes fraught when the individual practitioner makes choices that lead to their own burnout and strain collaboration across departments.

Instead of seeing resources as limited, skilled me teams are open to navigating design through resources. Individual practitioners actively dissect the scripted needs and listen to concepts, and producer or director goals, and arrive at visual and technical solutions well-served by their own expertise. Best practice for design and technical practitioners on a me team is to engage in conversation around concepts and essentials being requested by collaborators. Often, the specificity of a request from an individual outside of your area of expertise is actually an attempt to pitch a solution to a problem. Distilling down to the actual problem, synthesizing it through your expert lens, and pitching a solution that takes into account the creative impulse as well as feasibility is of utmost importance to the me team. This allows for all interdisciplinary collaborators to contribute, but for the solution, which will be carried out by the solo practitioner, to be under their purview and to not cause harm to the collective by creating overwhelm, avoiding an inappropriate solution that results in continued issues and buildup of work.

Me teams are formed by producing organizations hoping to engage in collaborative work that is fully produced, but may be lacking in the resources to flesh out departments with multiple practitioners. There may or may not be a full understanding within the organization of the multiple hats one practitioner is being asked to wear. While educating producing organizations can lead to realistic expectations, there is also acceptance expected on behalf of the practitioner that they are engaging in work without the flexibility to request additional team members, so all tasks required to produce the scale of work desired will need to be completed successfully by oneself. It is important at the outset of the contracting phase that the practitioner understands the expectation of the producing organizations. A me team is unlikely to be able to produce a work of Broadway proportions. As the visually trained experts in their fields, me teams often strive for a greater quality than resources indicate. Doing so should be the choice of the practitioner as opposed to an expectation of the producing organization. Teams of this type often engage in these projects either as portfolio and skill-building opportunities, or because a particular project ignites passion.

Successful workload management relies on a deep understanding of tasks and time. Many me teams are comprised of early career professionals who lack this depth of understanding. Proceeding with caution before over-designing and drilling down to what is necessary starts the workload management process off in the right direction. This combined with creative problem solving and out of the educational box thinking will lead to successful completion of goals.

Chances are when working in this scale of production, collaborators will have day jobs. They must be cognizant of time dedicated to the show while fulfilling their other responsibilities. In the

United States it is likely that you will be employed as an independent contractor, possibly without a written contract. This can cause personal liabilities if something goes wrong and someone gets hurt. There are also tax implications, good and bad as a contractor. Before agreeing to work with these employment particulars, the smart "me" will understand these details. If you work in this type of contract system often it is worth forming a Limited Liability Company (LLC), rules vary by state so check with a local lawyer or accountant.

On me teams, an individual practitioner wears many hats in order to conceptualize a design and bring it to fruition. On functional teams, akin to what one might find in LORT theatre, there are many practitioners who contribute to set or costume departments. The larger the team, the narrower the focus an individual has. By looking at all the hats possible within set and costume departments, an individual practitioner can get specific about what couple of hats they will wear while being a team of one, with an eye towards what they are actually capable of and what the show needs. If one isn't able to build a flat, well maybe this is about developing a set concept that integrates found materials. If one has the skill to construct a garment from a pattern, then maybe you are positioned to have a built costume design, but time and compensation should be considered.

SET AND COSTUME TEAMS

To bring a set design to fruition, expertise is needed in the areas of scene design, set engineering and fabrication, scenic art, properties, and stage operations. To bring a costume design to fruition, expertise is needed in the areas of costume design, costume construction, crafts, hair and makeup, and wardrobe. Regardless of how many practitioners are on the team, expertise is needed in all these aforementioned areas. When teams are large, there are departments staffed with expert individuals who work collaboratively inside and across departments to complete the work. All practitioners in these departments rely on hard skills from the same categories: analytic abilities, creative techniques, transformational processes, investigatory research, operational skills, and negotiation tactics. The hard skills within the ACTION category narrow to meet the demands of the specific jobs. However, the DIRECT (dependability,

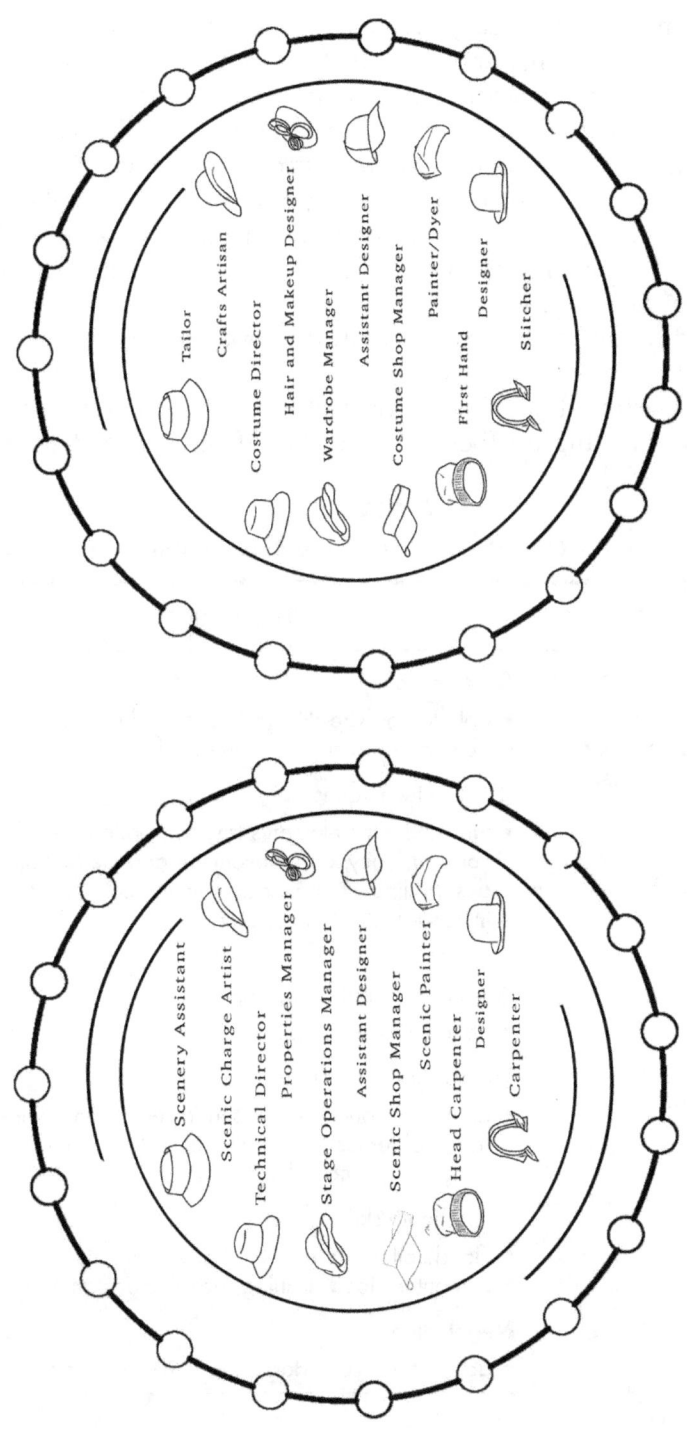

FIGURE 2.1 Me Team Hats.

interpersonal communication, respect, emotional intelligence, critical thinking, and transparency) soft skills remain consistent regardless of position. Set practitioners rely on their soft skills to navigate many different kinds of teams, both large and small, where they either contribute in a focused area of strength, or wear many hats. Individuals must achieve competency, and strive for excellence in their hard skills in order for production objectives to be met. But it is the use of soft skills that allows the objectives to be met in a positive collaborative atmosphere.

Hard skills related to the distinct departments are given in Table 2.1.

A department-specific set or costume team member wears a hat that is in a highly focused lane. Free from the distraction of

TABLE 2.1

ACTION Hard skills by department

DEPARTMENTS (HATS)	HARD SKILLS
Scene design • Designer • Associate designer • Assistant designer	**A**nalytic ability • able to analyze dramatic texts and read music • able to organize and present information **C**reative techniques • implement the elements (rhythm, pattern, emphasis, contrast, unity, and movement) and the principles of design (line, shape, space, value, color, and texture) in service of the stage picture • draw, draft, paint, and model build **T**ransformational processes • able to render an idea in an architectural scale **I**nvestigatory research • able to conduct and present research on a wide range of topics, especially related to period styles, geography, and cultures **O**perational skills • cloud collaboration, word processing • computer aided drafting, graphic design **N**egotiation • accounting, calendars, deadlines, leadership

Set engineering and fabrication
- Technical director
- Associate technical director
- Assistant technical director
- Scene shop supervisor
- Assistant scene shop supervisor
- Lead carpenter
- Carpenters
- Scene shop shopper/buyer
- Lead rigger
- Riggers
- Automation specialist

Analytic ability
- able to interpret drawings
- able to comprehend artistic concepts
- able to organize and present information

Creative techniques
- integrate artistic concepts
- structural engineering
- draw and draft

Transformational processes
- make in full scale that which is drawn in an architectural scale

Investigatory research
- able to conduct and present research on a wide range of topics, especially materials and technologies

Operational skills
- cloud collaboration, word processing
- computer aided drafting, graphic design
- tool usage and safety

Negotiation
- accounting, calendars, deadlines, leadership

Scenic art
- Scenic charge artist
- Scenic artist
- Set painter

Analytic ability
- able to interpret drawings
- able to comprehend artistic concepts

Creative techniques
- integrate artistic concepts
- color mixing and matching
- detailed drawing and cartooning (simplified drawing)

Transformational processes
- enlarging artwork from rendering to drop, scenic unit, etc.
- paint and texture applications

Investigatory research
- able to conduct and present research on materials and technologies

(Continued)

TABLE 2.1 *(Continued)*

DEPARTMENTS (HATS)	HARD SKILLS
	Operational skills • able to use brushes, rollers, sprayers, drawing tools, etc. • cloud collaboration, word processing **N**egotiation • accounting, calendars, deadlines, leadership
Properties • Props manager • Assistant props manager • Props carpenter • Props artisan/technician • Props painter	**A**nalytic ability • able to analyze dramatic texts and read music • able to organize and present information **C**reative techniques • implement the elements (rhythm, pattern, emphasis, contrast, unity and movement) and the principles of design (line, shape, space, value, color, and texture) in service of the elements • draw, draft, paint, and make plans **T**ransformational processes • make what is presented on scaled drawings or through research into objects that actors can interact with • combine raw and found materials to represent specific objects or design **I**nvestigatory research • able to conduct and present research on a wide range of topics, especially related to period styles, geography, and cultures **O**perational Skills • cloud collaboration, word processing • computer aided drafting, graphic design **N**egotiation • accounting, calendars, deadlines, leadership
Stage operations • Stage operations supervisor • Deck lead • Props runner	**A**nalytic ability • understand cue sheets and production paperwork **C**reative techniques • ability to seamlessly integrate work into a larger system **T**ransformational processes • animate scenery and props as needed, in a specific time frame or rhythm

- Technicians:
  - Deckhand
  - Fly rail operator
  - Etc.

Investigatory research
- understands venue
- understands staffing needs

Operational skills
- cloud collaboration, word processing
- tool usage and safety

Negotiation
- calendars, leadership

DEPARTMENTS (HATS)	HARD SKILLS
Costume design • Designer • Associate designer • Assistant designer • Shopper	**A**nalytic ability • able to analyze dramatic texts and read music • able to organize and present information **C**reative techniques • implement the elements (rhythm, pattern, emphasis, contrast, unity and movement) and the principles of design (line, shape, space, value, color, and texture) in service of character creation • draw, paint and source **T**ransformational processes • ability to work proportion and understand movement **I**nvestigatory research • able to conduct and present research on a wide-range of topics, especially related to period styles, fashion, and cultures **O**perational skills • cloud collaboration, computer rendering, graphic design, word processing **N**egotiation • accounting, calendars, deadlines, leadership
Costume construction • Costume director • Associate costume director • Assistant costume director	**A**nalytic ability • able to interpret drawings • able to comprehend artistic concepts • able to organize and present information **C**reative techniques • integrate artistic concepts • draw, engineer, draft and drape

(Continued)

TABLE 2.1 *(Continued)*

DEPARTMENTS (HATS)	HARD SKILLS
• Costume shop manager • Assistant costume shop manager • Draper • Tailor • First-hand • Stitcher	**T**ransformational processes • ability to work in scale • interpretation, understanding of proportion, line, shape, space **I**nvestigatory research • able to conduct and present research on a wide-range of topics, especially materials and technologies **O**perational skills • cloud collaboration, computer aided drafting, graphic design, word processing • tool usage and safety **N**egotiation • accounting, calendars, deadlines, leadership
Craft • Lead crafts artisan • Crafts artisan • Painter/dyer • Milliner	**A**nalytic ability • able to interpret drawings • able to comprehend artistic concepts **C**reative techniques • color theory, interpretation, understanding of proportion, line, shape, space • integrate artistic concepts **T**ransformational processes • ability to work in scale **I**nvestigatory research • able to conduct and present research on a wide-range of topics, especially materials and technologies **O**perational skills • tool usage and safety **N**egotiation • accounting, calendars, deadlines, leadership
Hair and makeup • Hair/makeup designer • Hair/makeup lead • Hair/makeup crew	**A**nalytic ability • able to analyze dramatic texts and read music • able to organize and present information

Transformational processes
- ability to work in scale

Investigatory research
- able to conduct and present research on a wide range of topics, especially related to period styles, geography, and cultures

Operational skills
- cloud collaboration, graphic design, word processing

Negotiation
- accounting, calendars, deadlines, leadership

Wardrobe
- Wardrobe manager
- Lead dresser
- Dresser
- Wardrobe day crew

Analytic ability
- interpret cue sheets and production paperwork

Creative techniques
- ability to seamlessly integrate work into a larger system

Transformational processes
- quick changes as needed, in a specific time frame or rhythm
- appropriate maintenance of garments to preserve desired effect

Investigatory research
- understands venue
- understands staffing needs

Operational skills
- safety, speed, and interpersonal skills
- cloud collaboration, word processing

Negotiation
- calendars, leadership

---

doing a little bit of everything, the member can hone their art and craft and achieve masterful results. Practitioners in each category strive for end results. A result can be accomplished in many different ways based on where a practitioner is in their training and the artist's preference. The feel or message of the play at hand can drive the techniques used to make the set. A solid pre-production process will lead to a product that will be integrated, run, and maintained by the stage operations team from tech through closing night. The table below illustrates the work required by project leads and their teams, stemming from the above departments. The me team model requires an understanding of all the normative tasks that fall to all departments, and necessitates strategic planning so that all outcomes are met.

TABLE 2.2

Processes and outcomes by hat – set team

HATS	PROCESSES	OUTCOMES
Set designer	Text analysis, connotative and denotative research, envision, drawing, drafting, modeling, monitoring, revision	THE WHAT Aesthetics Scaled plans
Technical director	Text analysis, material research, drafting, budgeting, scheduling, purchasing, installing, striking, planning	THE HOW Engineering Build drawings
Lead carpenter	Measuring, cutting, assembling, finish work, cleaning – follow plans	THE MAKING Structure
Scenic charge artist	Material research, budgeting, scheduling, purchasing, priming, layering, sealing, cleaning – follow plans	THE FINISH Surface treatment, Color and texture
Properties manager	Text analysis, list making, budgeting, purchasing, finding, modifying, crafting, replenishing, maintaining	THE SPECIFICS Objects
Run crew	Text analysis, paperwork, preparation, interaction with performers, preset pieces, respond to cues	THE RUN

TABLE 2.3

Processes and outcomes by hat – costume team

HATS	PROCESSES	OUTCOMES
Costume designer	Text analysis, connotative and denotative research, envision, drawing, rendering, sourcing, budgeting, monitoring, revision	THE WHAT Aesthetics Renderings Sourcing Paperwork

Shop manager	Text analysis, estimating labor and materials, hiring, managing workflow, scheduling, list making, sourcing, communicating	THE WORKFLOW Organization Personnel What's possible?
Draper/Tailor/ Patternmaker	Text analysis, project planning, materials research, engineering, drafting/draping, measuring, cutting	THE HOW & THE MAKING Engineering Patterns
First-hand/ Stitcher	Cutting, assembling, finish work, modifying, crafting	THE MAKING Constructing Finishing
Hair and makeup	Text analysis, connotative and denotative research, envision, drawing, rendering, sourcing, budgeting, styling, ventilating, revision	THE SPECIFICS
Run Crew	Text analysis, paperwork, preparation, interaction with performers, dressing, changing, laundering, maintaining	THE RUN

Me Team Set Activity

Creating a realistic-looking hardwood floor is a common requirement of a set design. Let's assume our collaborative interdisciplinary team is producing work in a traditional proscenium venue, staging a scene on an established playing area that is 16′ x 12′ wide. You, as a solo practitioner, are the set team.

What do you need to know about the venue before you can envision a plan?

- Brainstorm and articulate three questions.
- Set your own parameters based on a real or imagined space.

What are your strengths (or aspirational strengths) as a set practitioner?

- Name three practical skills you have that can serve set design.

Refer to the six hats from Table 2.2 and borrow a process from each relevant category to plan and execute the floor.

- Write down six unique processes you will use to bring the design to fruition.

- Write what steps would be involved in each process. Be specific as to how you would accomplish the tasks for the processes you have identified.

The play is opening, and you need an end result.

- What is your end result? (painted treatment, constructed element, found items, some combination, etc.)
- How much did it cost you?
- How much time did it take to complete?

Me Team Costume Activity

The three-piece suit is a common garment that spans western history and is often utilized by designers. The approach to a three-piece suit through sourcing or construction is predictably budgeted for by utilizing going rates. Assuming we have a me team working under ideal circumstances, we'll illustrate an example that utilizes the practitioner's design, technical and management skills to the extent appropriate. Starting with the given of an early 1930's pant, coat, and vest for a male identifying character, and a materials budget of $80, we will imagine the ideal cut is distinctly 1930's (wide leg pant, wide lapel) with a window-pane plaid. The team has culled through stock and come up short on the perfect suit. What would your approach be assuming this is a priority for the design?

What do you need to know about the venue before you can envision a plan?

- Brainstorm and articulate three questions for the producing team.

What are your strengths (or aspirational strengths) as a costume practitioner?

- Name three practical skills you have that can serve costume design.

Refer to the six hats from Table 2.3 and borrow a process from each relevant category to plan and execute the suit.

- Write down six unique processes you will use to bring the design to fruition.
- Write what steps would be involved in each process. Be specific as to how you would accomplish the tasks for the processes you have identified.

The play is opening, and you need an end result.

- What is your result? (constructed element, found suit, purchased suit, some combination, etc.)
- How much did it cost you?
- How much time did it take to complete?

PROCESS: PRE-PRODUCTION

In this scale of production, the conceptualization process does not always require the same techniques as larger scales; what works for you may or may not become a standardized process for the organization. Different techniques produce the same end result; streamline and efficiency, keeping in mind a quality outcome, are the name of this game at this scale. Since the designer is also the manager and fabricator, communication is centralized on sharing with collaborators outside your me team. It can be easy to stray from original design concepts due to the internal struggle between designer and maker. When making, stay true to your research and do not skip the process of identifying foundational visual anchors.

Many traditional training programs teach a process that begins with research and ends with a design package submitted to a shop. In the me team scenario, the practitioner is both designer and shop. So, deciphering what is essential to the pre-production process is advised. A highly detailed rendering of a costume illustrating the exact application of trim, closures, etcetera is mainly useful in shop collaborations. By contrast, in communicating with directors and fellow designers, the intention and emotion of the rendering is more effective. You might question, in the cases of purchasing an item, renting an element, or pulling from stock, if a drawing is necessary at all. Consider if sourcing of an actual prop during the pre-production process, thus running a parallel process of actualization to the conceptualization, would be a more effective use of time.

The notion that one must always conceptualize and then draw before entering real world possibilities doesn't necessarily work well when functioning as a "me." Opening yourself up to parallel processes that occur simultaneously, that need only take into account your own workload and parameters, is in service of accomplishing the work efficiently and effectively. In this way, the pre-production process and actualization phase are parallel processes. However, cutting corners on pre-production can result in problems onstage if certain considerations are not accounted for. Keep in mind that foundations create better outcomes when building any item from scratch, whether it is a scenic element or a costume. Embarking on a building process without specificity in a drawing will result either in safety concerns or a "two steps forward, one step back" process. Always engage in the full process when necessary, but ask oneself if there are efficiencies that can be relied on in those processes that are beneficial to balancing the many hats you are wearing. For example, what technologies exist to facilitate faster or more accurate drawings? Are there alterable stock items in existence in a theatre's storage or in the form of a commercial pattern? Has this trick been attempted at another theatre this size, and is there an open-source write-up for reference?

Even in a me team process, it is useful in the planning of productions to place resource numbers on a project or idea. These numbers may be a time commitment or a price - this paint treatment will take eight hours, that curtain will cost $300, the wise team member will plan for these parameters and stick with them. This is how productions are built in time for opening and on a budget. Large scale productions require a formalized and communicated budget methodology, small scale allow for nimble changes. As the sole practitioner in your area, these changes are up to you to make. If a particular element is important and it will take more time than estimated, you may easily make the decision to stretch your time and accomplish that element to its fullest. By contrast, a detail that is less important can be skipped, or reduced in complexity, due to lack of resources, but any noticeable shifts should be communicated with the entire producing team so there are no surprises in what appears onstage.

Establishing priorities during pre-production is important. The scale and scope of the set and costume outcomes are often intentionally small or modern in nature when me teams are responsible. But rest assured that you can still leave your mark as a designer/technician even with limited resources. Concentrate on what moments, locations, or characters are key and speak to you as a designer. Focusing in on a few design touches that truly represent your aesthetic while working to functionally service the production can be a fulfilling as well as a sustainable approach that does not tax your ability to produce what you have designed.

PROCESS: ACTUALIZATION

Unlike our teammates in lighting and sound, costumes and scenery do the majority of their work before the actors enter the theatre. The fabrication of the sets and costumes will happen wherever possible and wherever the organization has space. It is common in these small teams for scenery to be built on stage, in the corner of a storage facility, or in a parking lot. Many me team artists bring work home with them and are able to have a fabrication space where they live. Think about those who live with you and be respectful that this is your work and passion, not theirs.

Planning is key to every actualization process. Just because you are a team of one and have no collaborators to communicate with or consider, doesn't mean planning is less important – logistics and scheduling still present challenges. Before engaging in the build, consider logistics – do not build the proverbial boat in the basement, only to find you have no support to get it up the stairs, and it doesn't fit through the door. Be forward thinking in the process of how and when you will complete tasks such as load in and fittings. Consider if there is an order that best serves you as an individual, while being mindful that it supports the needs of the production and intersects with the availability of the space while supporting the needs of the performers with whom you engage. Thinking this through reduces the number of repeated tasks. For example, if you are shopping a costume, on the first shopping trip out you should buy options for a performer, both in size and shape. In this way you will reduce the likelihood of needing to shop multiple times and schedule multiple fittings. One of the most difficult aspects of the me team is the ability to procrastinate or disregard planning altogether. There is virtually no one who this will impact on a daily basis other than yourself. However, the more chaotic or delayed the approach is to a particular task, the less likely an end production will be ready for the entire interdisciplinary production team's engagement, whether that includes the actors or the lighting designer. It should also be noted that we should care about the potential distress we cause ourselves.

Working by oneself can present an array of safety challenges. Be aware and make safety a priority. It may seem simple but never run power tools or climb ladders alone; think about a buddy system when walking to your vehicle late at night; check in with collaborators to ensure someone always knows if you are in the theatre by yourself.

In an ideal process, set and costume collaborators arriving at tech will bring a warm feeling of relief – the fabrication is finished and the addition of the actors proves that all the planning, thought, and creation was effective. This is not always the case and technical rehearsals can bring a wave of anxiety and difficult conversations, and that's OK. The key here is to put your health, safety, and well-being first. Most of the hard discussions are not personal, though they can feel that they are. A certain magic can occur in tech and this is where the best team comradery is often born – collaborators solve problems on the fly with the given resources of time, money, and people. Those who can support you at the last minute, and contribute to the making of meaningful art, become go-to team members and lifetime friends.

Working with the other me teams proves that interdepartmental conversations are necessary for production cohesion. It is a good reminder to break out of your discipline when you are part of a larger department.

At the me team scale, producers and managers need to think out of the box when it comes to tech schedules so that the "shop of one" has time to do the notes before the next call. Sets, costumes and props may all be used as imagined during tech, but discovery happens, and sometimes a change or addition is really needed. In some regards, revisions at this scale are simplest, because those making the choices are executing them – there are no over hire painters to schedule, no milliners to fly in, there is only what the "me" has the time and skill to accomplish that will be addressed.

PROCESS: THE RUN

Stage management is the communication conduit (and at this scale, sometimes a board operator), once the show is running. Production reports are the best way for designers and technicians to know how a show went and if work needs to be accomplished before the subsequent shows. It's very important these reports make their way out as soon as possible, and that timely responses are given, since a teammate's day might change drastically if a production item is damaged, and a repair is needed. In the age of smart phones, communication has become very efficient.

And guess what, if there is anything set/paint/props to be maintained, it's you! If a costume needs repair, it's you who has to fix it. Anticipate what the typical maintenance needs are, and hold the time to be available if needed, and get contracted to handle the notes that come up during the run.

When the production has reached the time for it to close; in small scale productions this is generally after a weekend or after a few weeks running, attention shifts to strike. It's possible the organization is renting a venue for the production so the me team production might not have a home; the collaborators might not have a designated venue with storage or access to a separate temperature-controlled storage facility. Contractually, the venue may need to be cleared by a specific time or additional charges may apply. Finding out where the items acquired and made for this production go at the end, including if they have a life beyond this production, is essential. Hopefully the organization can obtain storage, although depending on the location, storage may be costlier than repurchasing or rebuilding many of the elements.

Arranging for people, vehicles, dumpsters can all be complicated at this scale. It's possible the organization has one lump sum for your area so contractually the material, labor, and any other logistics are one budget line. It's important to remember that if you need to book the rental truck for strike, save time and budget to fill it with fuel before you return it – this detail can be easy to forget earlier in the process. It is imperative to reserve the budget for strike, and make sure the date is in your calendar.

CONCLUSION

The me team practitioner is not alone. They are part of a larger interdisciplinary collective of designer/technicians, directors, managers, and performers, as theatrical works are generated through combining and synergizing artistic ideas and talents; creating an end product that does not have individual ownership.

As we discuss set and costume teams further, we'll explore the me idea in the context of individuals taking ownership of specific tasks - to talk about who the buck stops with. When there is a large team within a single department, room is left for no one to take ownership of the decision-making, and for pieces of the project to fall through the task and not get done. Individuals on teams must fulfil the expectations of the hat they are wearing, and on a me team, they fulfil the expectations of several hats – they are wise to be clear with their collaborators about which hats they are wearing and define what hard skills will be deployed in service to the production.

Me Team Activity

This exercise is meant to empower the solo practitioner in their creative process by providing a framework for determining the scope of what is feasible in production scenarios where there is limited budget and personnel. This exercise easily works for any play title or musical book and score, but can also be applied to any performative work where various departments join forces to present a singular event and when a choreographic score, an outline of actions, or a devised process has led to a script-like document.

Overview

Imagine you are the sole set design practitioner or costume shop practitioner on an interdisciplinary team.

Imagine you are working on a production of *INSERT TITLE*, and budgets are modest.

Today's exercise is to get you to think about what "things" you should take responsibility for.

Main ideas:

- Time can drive scope and inform the design solution.
- Think outside the box when it comes to resources.
- Inventories impact feasibility.
- Options are important.
- Know when to outsource.

Step One: Visual Anchors

Research that informs how an environment or character should feel, rather than research or renderings that prescribe a solution, allows for there to be many right answers for the set and costumes in terms of visual solution. It can be a singular fine art image, a mood board, and gestural sketches that drive the design concept. Identifying good research imagery that has an emotional connection for you to the play is not a throw away exercise. Certainly, the internet has given tremendous access to resources, but expert practitioners dedicate appropriate time and due diligence to identifying the best possible sources.

- Determine three givens in the text, and work with a subject librarian to identify at least three books or digital sources that illuminate the givens through visuals. These givens may relate to people, places and things, or to what, where, and when.
- Assemble your finds through collage or gestural drawings, keeping source imagery on hand in both cases.
- In looking at the visuals, do you think the visual solutions for set and costumes will be realistic or abstract or a combination of the two? To what extent will the design elements concretely represent or evoke an idea? Discuss your rationale based on the source dramatic work (play, dance, etc.)

Step Two: Brainstorming Resources

When imagining the world and the characters, acknowledge that you have no help to make, find, or modify any tangible production values that are essential for storytelling.

Questions to ask:

- Is there an inventory you can access?
- Do you have any resources or networks that you can access to "stretch your dollar" or "maximize sustainability?"
- We're not imagining this as "poor theatre," so what labor/techniques must be outsourced given the

(Continued)

production requirements and your skill set? What does your visual anchor indicate?

Step Three: Determining Scope

There will only be one week of tech, so you need to be realistic about what can be accomplished in this amount of time YOU, as the designer/technologist/manager have. Make some calculations for yourself:

- How many scenes, how many transitions?
- How many are long, how many are short?
- Are sets and costumes changing at any points in the action?
- What kinds of "design integration" take up tech time?

The steps above benefit from discussion, but certainly can be points of self-reflection.

Step three can be used as a "pair, think, share" exercise with collaborators from distinct departments.

These steps serve as a foundation for a paper project that exercises the individual practitioner's ability to find concrete solutions, with an eye towards there being more than one right solution to a creative problem.

- Identify three things specific for your discipline that reappear more than once in the production and are integral to storytelling and complex in some way. Describe the thing and its function; know what scenes the things are in. Discuss these three specific things in a short essay – a paragraph for each thing.
- Make three research pages. Each page contains three distinct images for each thing; star your favorite piece of research for each thing. The starred image should inform a design solution.
    - Image 1: research from a book or digital source
    - Image 2: photo of piece from stock or online marketplace
    - Image 3: your choice
- Find a book that supports the visual dramaturgy of the production; this book must be from your local library and must be brought to a pin-up day; images

from the book must inform at least one of your three things.
- Provide a "resource study" for the most challenging of your starred items. A resource study should include notes of the following:
  o notes on acquisition and/or fabrication
  o notes on personnel required for acquisition and/or fabrication
  o notes on materials and inventory to be incorporated
  o notes on hidden costs
  o notes on the rehearsal process related to the thing
  o notes on tech process related to the thing

INDUSTRY PERSPECTIVE: AN INTERVIEW WITH SCENIC DESIGNER CHELSEA WARREN

Chelsea M. Warren (she/her) is a multimedia artist with a focus on scenic and puppet design, as well as large scale photography and art installations. As a scenic designer she has worked at companies including Steppenwolf Theatre, Ananya Dance Theatre, Jungle Theater, Penumbra Theatre, Victory Gardens, Studio Theatre, Philadelphia Theatre Company, Cleveland Play House and Steep Theatre. As a puppet designer she has worked at Chicago Shakespeare Theatre, Studio Theatre, Jungle Theater, WaterTower Theatre and Skokie Valley Symphony Orchestra. She was the recipient of the Michael Maggio Emerging Designer Award. Ms. Warren received her MFA from Northwestern University and is an Assistant Professor of Scenic Design at the University of Minnesota Twin Cities.

In terms of what makes a collaboration successful, what comes to mind, first and foremost?

I've recently been writing a paper on a class that I taught at Columbia College Chicago, where I previously taught. The class has partner instructors of a director and a design team. In that class we investigated and codified "the circle method." In a successful collaboration, you're all in a circle holding space for the work in the middle.

This space exists when we're all working towards that goal of creating the work in the middle; nobody is taking over the center. The director is holding space to make sure that everyone is contributing, and we're all working in this circular collaborative way to make the work in the center better. I think it is rare when all people are equally standing together, but it's exciting when that happens, and the work is better because everyone's contributing.

What communication tactics work, specifically for you, in the context of your organization or your process in general?

I try to cater my communication based on the communication preferences of the participants I'm working with. For example, I note that some people do better in a group conversation, and I enjoy that because then everyone is hearing the same conversation. I know that there are certain collaborators that don't like having big conversations in front of people, so I try to be flexible. Is this a one-on-one versus a group conversation? I'm constantly thinking through those things. To have my voice or opinion heard, is it going to work better in the group, or would one on one be more successful? Or, with visual communication, I observe is this a director that can understand ideas based on ground plans or research, or is a model the most helpful?

What's the breath of scale and types of organizations that you tend to do design work in?

I liked considering this question, because I originally built my career in Chicago starting off in very small theatres where we had no budget. There was this big moment in my trajectory in which a director I work with regularly and I got a show where we had a budget that to us was just so much money, but everyone kept telling us at the organization, you "only have x budget". To us, that x budget was the golden ticket, to that company it was a pittance. It's interesting to think about as I grew, the scale grew. The scale I was working on at the smaller storefront theatres had a different focus. I loved that I could focus on the performer and spectator experience because it's so intimate. A lot of what I'm doing as a designer is shaping that experience; creating the arena that the story is told in. When there's not much I can contribute visually because this space and resources are small, I can make a few specific choices that animate the storytelling.

Whereas now I have the privilege of working at larger institutions where an exciting part is getting to collaborate with artisans who make the work better. I love collaborating with artists like scenic painters and technical directors who elevate my ideas. I'm drawn to both scales because when you're at the bigger organizations, often your productions must be friendly to a wider audience. There's less risk-taking in terms of what plays are being produced. Not always, but sometimes the material is not as exciting as the little storefront theatres that are producing the boldest pieces.

Can you tell us about a time when you were a member of an interdisciplinary team, where you were the only specialist in your area of design/technology expertise, and the efforts resulted in a performative work arrived at through collaboration? What was the outcome of your efforts? What was a method or technique used in that particular process that bettered the outcome? What can others learn from this success in order to better their own practice as an interdisciplinary team member?

As a puppet designer I almost always have to make the puppets myself. I made the dragon for *Shrek the Musical* at Chicago Shakespeare Theatre. It was soon after *Warhorse* had happened on Broadway and the director was interested in the puppet having a quality similar to those horses. There was a natural reed skeletal structure so that we could see into the makings of the puppet. The production's design concept overall had an exposed quality.

This one is a great example because I was the maker, and it was a new technique for me to learn. Although I had done similar things, I was working with new fabrication techniques to shape the armature out of natural materials. Additionally, the dragon had lit up eyes and smoke came out of her nose. I was able to work with other artists to make these effects happen. The head electrician, and their assistant took care of the lit up eyes. I talked them through my construction of the huge head and together we discussed the best casing and cabling placements. For the fog machine that made the smoke, I had to build the snout in such a way that we could fit a mini fog machine and provide access to load the fogger for each show.

During preview performances the puppet had some technical hiccups like the head disconnecting from the neck and together with the technical director we went over some of the joints and made some safety decisions – I thus learned about how to use aircraft cable as safety loops. I got to work with all these different technicians, who helped make the puppet cooler – all the tricks that happened, and ultimately, it looked like a cohesive puppet.

What unique and/or essential tool, low-tech or high-tech, aided the "making" of the design?

For me, the unique tool is constantly going back to storyboarding and thinking through on paper what is the storytelling and what is the vision – what are the visual sequences of events that I want to tell? It is essential to return to the design process when making decisions, figure it out all on paper, and then construct it.

Another key that has been essential in not wasting my own time is communicating with people that know more than me. For example, and I don't know how this happened, but I had never corn starched a drop before, and I needed to do it with no space to do it. So, I talked to the technician at my school and got advice. I ended up doing it in the backyard and at first, I didn't get the mixture quite right, but I learned and it was super fun to have all of these mini puppet drops drying in the backyard.

What types of performative work lends themselves to having individuals, working as the sole designer/technician in their area of expertise, join forces to make a single theatrical event? Why do you think this is, and how do you find this kind of work?

I look towards devised theatre. In Chicago I was a part of a devised theatre company called Yellow House. In that group, I often ended up being the projection designer, because we worked in site specific places where a set wasn't as needed. Also, there actually was another set design collaborator, because we began the company with, "choose cool artists that we want to have in the room working together." We made a number of pieces.

One of our pieces was at a site-specific abandoned building on the North Shore on Lake Michigan. The space had these huge pillars throughout a big shell cement building. People could slip behind huge pillars and be gone. It was an old pumping station with large open window holes and beyond them was Lake Michigan. When we did the site-specific version, we created a vocabulary for the piece where a person would hide behind a pillar and disappear and then reappear at another point and people could jump outside of the window or jump in from the windows as entrances. When we translated it to a black box version of the show, there were many collaboration conversations. We had spent so much time in the site-specific space, we spent days there observing how does light affect this place at different times of day. We scheduled our film shoot based on that sun. We brought all of that into the theatre; one of the biggest questions we had to first tackle was the windows. Should the windows be open portals for entrances or exits, or visual story telling surfaces? One of the things that I loved about the onsite windows were that you could see on one side trees with leaves blowing, and on the other side waves coming in and out on the shore. I advocated for hanging fabrics that were the portals of the windows. I could then project from behind onto these hanging rectangles and you could see the environment shifting. We were able to achieve an emotional shifting world rich with symbolism. I changed the mood of the space based on the quality and reality of the projection. It was magical in terms of recreating the site specific in a black box setting, heightening the most essential parts and placing them into a theatre.

When you are the sole practitioner realizing the set design, what do you consider to be must do steps in both the creative process and realization phase of the work?

Making sure that I allow myself the dreaming phase with the collaboration team. Sometimes there can be the tendency to skip that because you're going to be the builder, so you don't need to do as much pre-planning. Dreaming and pre-planning are two separate steps. It's crucial to allow that time to dream as a group and try to avoid thinking about the hours that each idea is going to take. Dream first and then figure out what is essential.

In terms of being my own my own fabricator, schedules, to do lists and sharing those deadlines with other people are all crucial. It's easy to get lost in the weeds of your own project, but if you know that you have the schedule you have to adhere to, that keeps you on track.

Is there a time when your design approach acknowledged yourself as the labor force to make the scenic elements?

When I am working with the dance company Ananya Dance Theatre, I heavily consider the resources and constraints. This specific company creates pieces on social justice issues from history, so I like to start with a deep dive into research. Based on the research, I focus on what is evocative and work with the parameters of both the piece and the resources. In my practice of designing for dance, when I am moving towards ideation, I am being much more practical. I look for tools and tricks to help me achieve the evocative while ensuring that no one is overburdened. In this example, the company also tours so everything must fit into about four snow board bags which is another layer of parameters.

In the last piece I designed, there was an altar that needed to hold ten specialty objects that were placed on it during the dance. I hired an assistant to come in and help me with props. The trick was the altar needed to be large enough that it could be seen from the audience, yet small or collapsible enough to fit into the snowboard bags. My assistant suggested that we start by looking at Ikea for things that exist that we could make into the artistic vision. We spent a while on different websites including Ikea, looking for framework.

It was a great idea, but I had such cool research that I decided I would take a week to work on this object myself and make the ideal piece. For me, a chicken wire base covered in fabric that held the specialty objects was important to my design. Having those conversations really makes you decide whether an idea is important or not. Early on, I designed a piece for this company about the silk trade. The backdrops were important to me, so I stitched fabric backdrops that they toured with. That element and its visual impact was important enough for me to put in the work myself, knowing it would require a lot of my time. It's a decision of weighing the practical solutions that are less time consuming or making the exact right singular object.

FIGURE 2.2 Ananya Dance Theatre.

O'Shaughnessy Auditorium (St Paul, MN) & International Tour; October 2021 Scenic Design: Chelsea M. Warren. Production Photography: Isabel Fajardo, Bruce Silcox

INDUSTRY PERSPECTIVE: AN INTERVIEW WITH COSTUME DESIGNER CAITLIN CISEK

Caitlin Cisek (she/her) is a designer, and visual artist. With an immense love for telling stories – and how textiles, technology, found objects, and even social media can all contribute to exciting visual communication, Caitlin has designed opera, film, theatre, dance, and new media. Her favorite work is the *Huddled Masses Project*; an editorial on identity and immigration. She earned a BA in Theatre from the State University of New York at Albany and MFA from the University of California, Irvine, and is currently working on her dissertation in Fashion and Textiles at The Royal Melbourne Institute of Technology. Caitlin is a proud member of United Scenic Artists Local 829.

What makes a collaboration successful?

The central idea being not only agreed upon, but really valued. It's been most successful for me when I know if the story or concept brought into the room in the first place is really valued – that the design team has taken the themes and concepts, and they are acknowledged consistently across the departments. I think that that allows for individual designers to make independent choices, and to explore ideas and inspirations in a way that doesn't feel like it's confrontational or antagonistic to another designer, and also doesn't feel like you're always giving something away in terms of design intention – designers can feel like we're exchanging priorities. For instance, if I want this to happen then I'm going to need to give this up, but that doesn't feel negative if you are always operating from the central idea. And, especially if you like that idea, then it actually becomes validating because as a designer you are creating something beautiful around the story.

As an example, I worked with a sound designer very closely on core data, costumes, and music for a show and they came in at one point, and one of those cues had gone in a wildly different direction. I remember feeling the frustration of having built a costume that was no longer relevant, but the change was so rooted in the idea that we both valued, that I was surprised at how quickly my annoyance went away, and I was able to focus on how right the change was. Of course, I made that designer buy me a drink! But when you hold the intention close, collaboration flows.

What communication tactics work specifically for you?

The cheeky but true answer is high speed wi-fi. Otherwise, in terms of communication, there are always people on the team who have the words, and there are always people on the team who have the pictures. And that translation always feels borderline impossible. For me, being able to respond to their words with pictures and always being able to adapt new ideas with visual images has been a really helpful tool in terms of actually understanding the people with the words, because they often can't fully explain using words and I often feel there is no other way to come together than through a quick visual image or multiple images – sometimes it means like I want this, but I want that color with this detail. It adds a level of specificity I can't capture in words.

What draws you to working on projects on the me team scale?

I think there are two answers – I think initially it's opportunity, especially when you're starting out. Not only do you not have access to places where you're going to have that shop support, but getting those places to believe in what you're doing is hard. It's hard because unless you come in with a fleshed-out resume, it's really hard to get other people to believe in your ideas. Especially when you're a younger designer, and you probably haven't totally figured out what you're doing because the reality is you know so little.

The other thing that is attractive is you don't have to ask for permission to pursue an idea. I would think: "yes I'm going to buy these four fabrics and then I'm going to glue them together and then we're going to slash them, dye them and fit them to an actor." The team would be on board because at this scale we are all united in making artwork. There was no one to ask "Well, have you thought it through? Do you know what dye bath time you need? Etc. etc." All of which serves to undermine my enthusiasm for the adventure.

So, I was attracted to it because I could take risks, and then I also had time and space to hide my mistakes –there would be no superior shop manager to point out how it didn't work or after the fact tell me what I should have done. If it didn't work, I could just throw it in the garbage and start over. It's about being able to experiment more freely and build your own trust in your design ideas, and I think that is why I pursued these contracts initially.

Can you tell us about a time when you were a member of an interdisciplinary team, where you were the only specialist in your area, and the efforts resulted in a performative work arrived at through collaboration? What was the outcome of your efforts? What was a method or technique used in that particular process that bettered the outcome? What can others learn from this success in order to better their own practice as an interdisciplinary team member?

This is such a cliché, but it was summer stock and I'm designing *A Midsummer Night's Dream*. Because isn't that all the nightmare we're living in all the time? I couldn't rent or order anything in time that resembled a structured underskirt. So, I ended up going to Home Depot and buying plastic sheeting of various strengths to cut into pieces and assemble into a skirt. The original iteration didn't work but that experiment informed other materials I bought to solve the problem. I ended up making medium grade plastic work like plastic boning. It was strong enough to support the skirt and translucent enough that I was able to put details inside of it so that it appeared objects were floating in the skirt. As an added bonus, it was plastic I could glue to it which was perfect because naturally I didn't have the time to delicately stitch the petticoat.

It was a great solution, but I'm reasonably sure I couldn't locate that product in Home Depot today because I shopped in a fever. However, it made me much more conscious of supplies that could be useful in costumes that are typically associated with scenery. But, I was proud of it. I'm still proud of it.

What unique and/or essential tool, low-tech or high-tech, aided the "making" of the design?

Honestly the tools that have been really helpful are wardrobe tools. I learned from my occasional work in television or film that they are often dependent on solutions that happen right now to go on camera. So, I started carrying those tools into theatre spaces - particularly a ring sizer and double stick tape. I could work more efficiently and with a better process with these tools. A simple ring sizer allows for more information to be gathered from the actor, and the temporary solutions double stick tape can provide can completely change the anxiety in the room. An actor's hem will be up for the night, but I don't have to run around attempting to fix it immediately. I think there is this undercurrent where we train to fix it now, and I don't know if that is necessary. Tape is ok temporarily and the hem will still be there tomorrow but won't cause anxiety tonight.

What types of performative work lend themselves to having individuals, working as the sole designer/technician in their area of expertise, join forces to make a single theatrical event? Why do you think this is, and how do you find this kind of work?

New works – when the entire team, including the playwright to some extent, is getting in on the ground level of the collaboration. With most new work you are often a shop of one, but you are working with a team of people who share that position in their area, and approach the work fresh. It allows you to let your guard down a bit. When you are the only team of one, or approaching work that isn't to the scale of a team of one, you aren't comfortable with how the team might receive a mistake. In those teams, there is a bit of performance in the room. Captaining that ship means not losing your cool. But, with new work, we are all experiencing the story for the first time and struggling to connect and create. I don't think that a degree of privacy is essential, and you can bond over that anxiety or learning curve.

Right now, I am working on a project composed of several costume designs for one performer. It's on a smaller scale, and on shoot day when things go wrong, being on a team of one has allowed me to be close to the details. When you are closer to the details and nuances, you are more invested in it. It's similar with new works.

When you are the sole practitioner realizing the costume design, what do you consider to be the must do steps in both the conceptual process and actualization phase of the work? Could you talk a little bit about some of the mechanics of your process? Does it range greatly?

From the beginning, I try to be mindful of not designing something I can't make. It doesn't always work out because I do think for the theatre artist there's no such thing. We assume we can always figure it out.

I am actually a big believer in habit – I allow certain parts of the process to be easy-going and unemotional. So, at the outset, I sit down with a script and multiple multicolor highlighters so that as I read, I can look for patterns and denote those visually.

In looking for patterns I understand that if a scene makes eight references to nature, and then subsequent scenes also have references to nature, I take that as a direction. This makes things clear and less intellectual for me, which is comforting because I know I haven't laid on meaning that isn't there. To denote these patterns visually can really help the team understand how I have arrived at the themes. To begin the research and drawing processes, I will often start with basic ideas – like prepare my plate with my signature, IATSE stamp, the character name, etcetera. All of the things that don't take internal commitment but prepare you emotionally for the work.

How do you manage your time when you are producing your own designs? Do you think about the amount of time you are giving different parts of the process along the way?

Well, in the beginning, I didn't manage it. But now I try to remain mindful of my time and how it is best spent. For example, we all assume we are supposed to be in rehearsal. But I often ask myself if I really need to be in this rehearsal. I think this often happens with costumes. There is a point in the process where scenery, lighting and sound have to be together to move forward. They have to be in the room. So, if I am invited into that room with the expectation that work is still happening, and costumes will be done, I try to be mindful of whether being in that room is the best use of my time. As a "me," if I am not working on the costumes, no one is.

For a long time, I didn't acknowledge this, and I tried to be everywhere. I don't do that anymore and for me mindfulness is time management.

Are there any hacks that you could offer for good time management?

One hack or habit I can offer, and I can't believe as a New Yorker I'm going to say this, but have a commute. A commute forces you to have time to decompress – it removes you from the space.

Often designers have creative space in their homes. Make sure there is a mechanism that physically removes you from your workspace during the day. Go to lunch if you work from home. I went back and forth on this for a while, because if I pack a lunch its cheaper, but I would also never leave the space. But if I went to a café, between the walk there, the ordering and eating, and the walk back, I would leave the building for 45 minutes. Those breaks are important because otherwise the overall fatigue will impact not only what you get done in a day, but how well you do it. When you take a break, it allows you the space to think.

Do you have any techniques for collaborating with the director to communicate expectations?

The short answer is I communicate with a smile. Requests often come with tension and can feel like a bomb that needs to be diffused. How a team reacts to that bomb is important. So, I tend to use a smile and humor to diffuse the situation so that we can have an honest conversation with the team's values in mind.

It's all about negotiation and setting priorities. When asked for something it's fine to say "yes we can absolutely do that" but usually there is a follow-up because of resources. If we do that, then we likely can't do something else. If the requests are both of value, the director or producer will come up with the resources whether it's delaying a rehearsal for more time or paying another person.

Do you think that this technique of deflecting and using humor is partially a defense mechanism as a woman – so that you are not perceived as aggressive?

Yes. 100%. I have hope that as we move forward it won't be necessary. But I found this tactic was natural for me, and worked in collaborative teams. It's turning lemons into lemonade, and I'm not advocating for that, but it is reality.

The thing about design is that the burnout rate is really high. The way to get past these behaviors and have a trusting collaboration is to work together repeatedly. But, the more you are doing on a project the less likely you are to have good relationships, because you are burnt out. If you don't have good relationships with a team or organization then you are less likely to get hired by them again and it becomes a cycle of burnout.

Once you have worked with a team or organization several times, these techniques for diffusing shouldn't be necessary. Trust between collaborators has been established and nothing that goes on in terms of setting expectations is going to be viewed as confrontational. It took me a long time to understand that the first time you work with anyone there isn't any trust. The first inkling of trust usually comes when the curtains go up on opening night.

When you are a one-person designer and shop, does that impact the way you relate to the performers?

I often forge the strongest bonds with actors in the me team scenario because we are getting a double dose of each other both as designer to actor and shop to actor. The hardest part is maintaining the line of process and professionalism. Sometimes, I feel like the characters in Star Wars who were stuck in the trash compactor. On one side is the ease of utilizing an actor's personal garment, on the other side is not wanting to lose control of the design aesthetic when the performer suddenly wants to bring in their own closet. It is a tightrope to walk. More often than not though, actors are pretty understanding and they want their costumes to succeed.

FIGURE 2.3 Huddled Masses Editorial, August 2020.
Costume Design: Caitlin Cisek

3
Self-managed Team

DEFINITION

The self-managed team for our purposes is composed of two–three collaborators in both the set and costume departments who are assembled on a project-to-project basis to make set and costume designs. They are contracted by the head of the producing organization and report to the artistic/producing director and in some instances, a production manager. This team is a staple of the small to midsize semi-professional companies and can be seen working in a diverse array of independent performing arts organizations that vary by city. Although these team members, the designers and technicians on the project, may be resident with the employing company, we assume there is not a shop head or other full-time staff member(s) whose work directly brings the set and costume designs to fruition. The members of the set and costume teams likely hold down other jobs, often full-time jobs within or outside of the discipline. The team members may be balancing many self-managed theatre projects at various stages of development synchronously, and in addition to the project at hand. They are decision makers as well as actual makers, and should be equally adept at handling highly technical challenges as they are willing to execute basic tasks. Given the time constraints and breadth of expertise of the small team, the self-managed team members may decide to send out a specific aspect of the design to be fabricated by an artisan, craftsperson, or business outside of the team. The cost of engaging additional makers generally comes out of the materials budget, and the person who performs the specialized tasks is not a core member of the team.

The self-managed team is often activated by a producing organization that has their own venue or the means to rent a venue for a dedicated amount of time. An artistic/producing director has determined the title and has brought on a director. The stage and/or scope of project is a decent size, and there is an ensemble cast, but the budget is modest, so a small team is contracted to actualize the designs. It's possible that a designer is sought out to work with the director and fellow designers to analyze the play, develop a visual approach to the storytelling, and be an active participant in physically realizing the design elements. It's assumed that the designer won't go it alone. The producing organization may have their own go-to collaborating technician for the set and costume departments independent of one another, or the designer may be asked to recommend a team member within the discipline – someone with a complimentary skill set. This isn't an exact science, and the technician may be brought on first – this is often the case when the scope of the production is known, and the crafts required and technologies that will be implemented have generally been pre-determined. Alternatively, a producing organization may contract an existing collaborative made up of practitioners with the scope of skill sets required for the artistic and technical challenges at hand. Although experts are often involved in the scope of production, the work is considered semi-professional as individual collaborators wear many hats and are often collaborating with emerging professionals or volunteer contributors.

FORM AND FUNCTION

If you're a designer or technician working on a self-managed team, theatre design and production is your calling or passion. You may be an emerging practitioner that is looking to be at the helm, you may be a seasoned professional who wants to remain active in a particular region, or maybe you were on high school stage crew and you just can't break the habit.

Performing arts organizations that engage self-managed teams produce for a wide range of reasons that include:

- showcasing new plays, musicals, and choreography
- reinvigorating classic dramatic works with fresh approaches
- serving the community by facilitating dialogues through performance
- providing a forum for artistic expression made by like-minded people

Typically, these organizations are not-for-profit and all parties who make the work understand that grant funding, donations, and projected ticket sales cover production expenses. Therefore, and in most cases, operating and production budgets are modest. The self-managed team understands that resources are a limiting factor in the making of the work. Some design ideas will not be possible, and some materials and specialized labor will not be affordable. The transparency of resources between the designer, technician and the organization can keep everyone on the same page, promote healthy collaboration across departments, and achieve an excellent outcome for all.

A key component to the self-managed team is the creation of work processes alongside the design and actualization of the production. Having little to no organizational management requires the team to develop practices for completing the work together. The responsibilities of the team will vary and will be determined by the team itself, but the members must be conscious of all the tasks that need to be divided and conquered including those that require working in unison. In the case of minimally supported productions, the designer and collaborating technician should make clear what aspect beyond studio design the designer will contribute, and what aspects beyond technical production the technician will contribute – all members need to know the hats they will be wearing. The designer may have more time invested at the top of the process while they find inspiration and meet with the director and develop a concept, where the technician may have additional responsibilities towards investigating inventories and managing a strike. Defining which hats each team member will wear should happen at the inception of the team.

As described above, chances are the designer on the self-managed team will contribute more than presenting a rendering or model and the essential paperwork package. The well-balanced self-managed team is the ideal - where the designer and the technician are even collaborators. Often, on the self-managed team, the designer may be viewed by the producer as the top of the team, but this is not necessarily the best practice. Ideally, the technician is seen as an even collaborator as they play a critical role as the keeper of feasibility and labor management, and without their "know how," the designs will not materialize. Vertical collaboration processes fall short of acknowledging the value each role brings to the team, create conflict, and can result in repeated efforts. While not every shift can be avoided by proper planning and collaboration, as a team redundancy can be reduced through circular collaborative structures.

The designer, technician, director, and producer are the primary stakeholders in the design concept and actualization. Does the environment work for the blocking, does the garment accommodate movement, are the visuals appropriate for the storytelling, can we engineer the idea, and do we have the time money and labor to actualize the concept are the primary concerns handled by these collaborators. Conflicts arise when a designer agrees to things that may not be possible with the given resources of a project or when the technician shuts down an idea without fully understanding the various permutations it could have. Horizontal communication between the designer and technician is important to avoid these issues, and the team members should view each other as equals. Compact teams make for efficient communication and nimble decision-making, and the self-managed team is poised to quickly confirm design decisions and adjustments as they occur.

No two self-managed teams are alike. At larger organizations, the designer may be the visitor and the technician may be contracted, with their contributions directed specifically to the realization. This leaves the designer to oversee and implement more artistic choice such as paint, props, or hair and makeup. If the scope of the production makes this untenable, it is possible for the team to educate the producers in how they would like to work within their organization, especially if they are creating their own team and bringing on their own collaborators.

The designer may negotiate a fee for an associate or assistant designer to meet the demands of the production in the given time frame, and in order to bring greater breadth of skills to the project. When assembling the self-managed team, consider the following questions to help determine the makeup.

- Will the set designer handle paint? Props?
- Will the costume designer handle makeup? Hair? Crafts?
- Who will handle modifications from rehearsal reports and during tech?
- Are there tasks the team does not have the skills to accomplish?

How these collaborations occur will wholly depend on organizational structure and if a self-managed team with equal contributors is possible. In some circumstances the designer will hire an artisan(s) or technician(s) to contribute as a subcontractor paid out of the design fee.

The ability to be upfront and concise about expectations, for instance what needs to be built by when, will avoid later conflicts. Having a level team, where the workload feels evenly shared, will be most successful and fulfilling for everyone.

SET TEAM

At minimum, a self-managed set team should be comprised of two members: the designer and the technician. This assumes that the set designer is capable of props design and scene painting, and that the technician will not only take the lead on scenic engineering and fabrication but be an active participant in any props artisan work that should arise. As the physical scale of set work can be large, and the work itself may involve heights and running industrious tools, there is often a third team member for purposes of handling scope, scale, and safety. This team size assumes the set is static or that any scene changes can be actuated by the actors or the stage management team. It also assumes that the maintenance of the show will be handled by the crew that is onsite for all performances, such as an assistant stage manager. This run crew member will handle paint touch-ups, minor repairs, and the purchase of expendable props such as food.

Contemporary set designers who receive formal training or who apprentice with seasoned designers are introduced to all facets of the set design discipline. The set designer will propose, render, and draft the environment for the performative experience at hand, but most have had practical training and active experience outside of the studio and in one or more of the following related fields:

- props design, fabrication, and management
- scene painting
- upholstery
- set construction and installation

This scope of training and experience has prepared them to engage throughout the production process – in the studio, in the "shop," and on stage. For a set designer to succeed on a self-managed team, they must be as comfortable around basic tools as they are at the drafting table. Designers working at this scale and on this kind of team can't

Self-managed Team 59

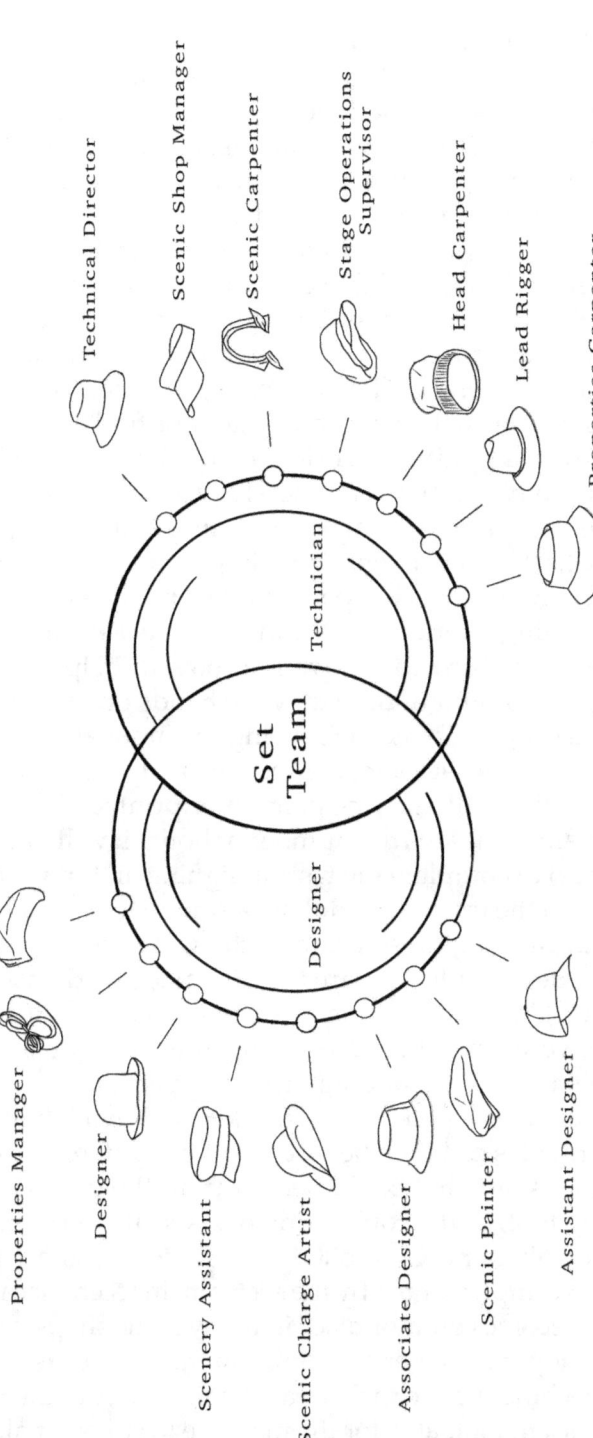

FIGURE 3.1 Self Managed Set Team Hats.

be afraid to get dirty. As they are usually expected to handle physical work including lifting weight, a designer should make the producing organization aware if accommodations need to be made.

The technician on a self-managed team usually has trained as a technical director or has experience as a theatrical carpenter. At this scale of production, it is rare to find the need and resources for metal fabrication. Steel and the tools required to work with it are costly and specialized. One will also find that extensive rigging is also rare in these types of venues, there may be a pipe grid or a few battens generally reserved for lighting, but anything beyond that will take several people to operate. The self-managed technical director will be very hands on with build and may not find a need for detailed working drawings and other documentation tactics which are rooted in communication between the TD and carpenters. For a technician to succeed on a self-managed team, they must have great communication skills, be open to engaging in the conceptual development of a project and be a very capable project manager.

When approaching work in the context of a self-managed team, collaborators may turn to innovative tools to help save on labor, minimizing the amount of time they are hands on with a particular aspect of the project. To decide if using the innovative tool is the best solution for the task at hand, a thorough analysis is in order. For instance, should the wallpaper be painted or printed? To arrive at an answer, the team compares the number of hours it will take the painter (set designer) to complete the task, assigning an hourly rate, plus material costs, to the number of dollars a square foot for a large format printer to print a high resolution of the wallpaper, plus the time it takes the set designer to prepare the digital art work (assigning an hourly rate). Practicalities such as the availability of large format printing in your area, the turnaround time, and quality of the wallpaper itself are all determining factors. If painting the wallpaper is the right answer – given time, money, and availability of resources, budget monies can then be reserved for a different aspect of the project, perhaps one that could benefit from the purchase or use of a time saving tool, or the contracting of a specific service.

The Computer Numeric Controlled (CNC) Router is a labor-saving tool that can be implemented by the set team. In recent decades, CNC Routers have become commonplace in many scene shops. In the absence of a scene shop, a designer or technician may form a relationship with a CNC machine shop in their area. There, a programmer will utilize software to assign toolpaths for the machine to cut on or along.

Many machines are capable of producing three-dimensional end products with more precision and speed than conventional means. Once the designer or technician has formed a relationship with an independent shop, they may fully integrate the machine into the workflow, and this tool can function to the level of having an additional carpenter. The capabilities will change the standards of structural design for the particular production. Arc and angular platform lids are cut by the CNC in lieu of router jigs and trigonometry. It is unlikely that the self-managed team would have their own CNC router, or that the company they are contracted by would, as the startup cost of the machine is significant (most entry level machines appropriate for scene shops are nearly $10,000), however the labor savings can be recouped quickly – if the organization's practitioners have the expertise to utilize and maintain the equipment. CNC routers need space, machine upkeep, and programming labor – they create noise and dust. For these reasons, the self-managed team should develop relations with local vendors that will take on CNC work at a per hour fee which can be an effective way of starting to use this labor-saving tool. Knowing when to utilize innovative tools and knowing when to seek expert support are signatures of good project management.

Self-managed Set Team Activity

As introduced in chapter 2, creating a realistic-looking hardwood floor is a common requirement of a set design. There is a wide range of techniques and materials that can create a hardwood floor, and assuming we have a self-managed team working under ideal circumstance, we'll illustrate an example that utilizes the designer's/painter's and technician's skill set equally. Starting with the given of the 16' x 12' platformed stage, we'll imagine that six 4' x 8' platforms can be pulled from the producing organization's stock, and that they will be legged up to eight inches. These platforms have been well-used and are showing their age, so covering the surface is required. The team notes that there are plenty of offcuts of lauan in stock, some of which is already primed. The lauan can be ripped into four-inch strips of various lengths to represent floor boards. There needs to be enough to cover the 192 square feet of surface. Three distinct paint colors are applied to the strips to emulate the wood grain. A semi-gloss sealant enhances the look.

- What tools does the set designer need?
- What tools does the technician need?
- How much lumber needs to be purchased?
- What hardware is required?
- How much time does it take to cut materials?
- How much time does it take to paint the boards?
- How much time does it take to assemble the stage?
- How much time does it take to lay the boards?
- What are "hidden" activities that take time?
- What are "hidden" costs?
- How much time and labor are required to make this platform stage with realistic hardwood treatment?

COSTUME TEAM

At minimum, a self-managed costume team should be comprised of three members: designer, technician, and wardrobe lead. This assumes each team member has basic skills in multiple facets of character design and creation and can therefore wear multiple hats. Character design and creation includes hair and makeup which is seldom separately addressed by organizations that establish self-managed teams.

Contemporary costume training, either through university or apprentice programs, introduces all facets of costume creation as a discipline. The costume designer will propose, render, source, and fit the costumes for the performative experience at hand, but most have had practical training and active experience outside of the studio and in one or more of the following related fields:

- costume construction
- costume crafts
- hair and makeup basics
- wardrobe

Similarly, costume technicians and wardrobe personnel have training across the discipline. Broadly, technicians manage and/or

Self-managed Team **63**

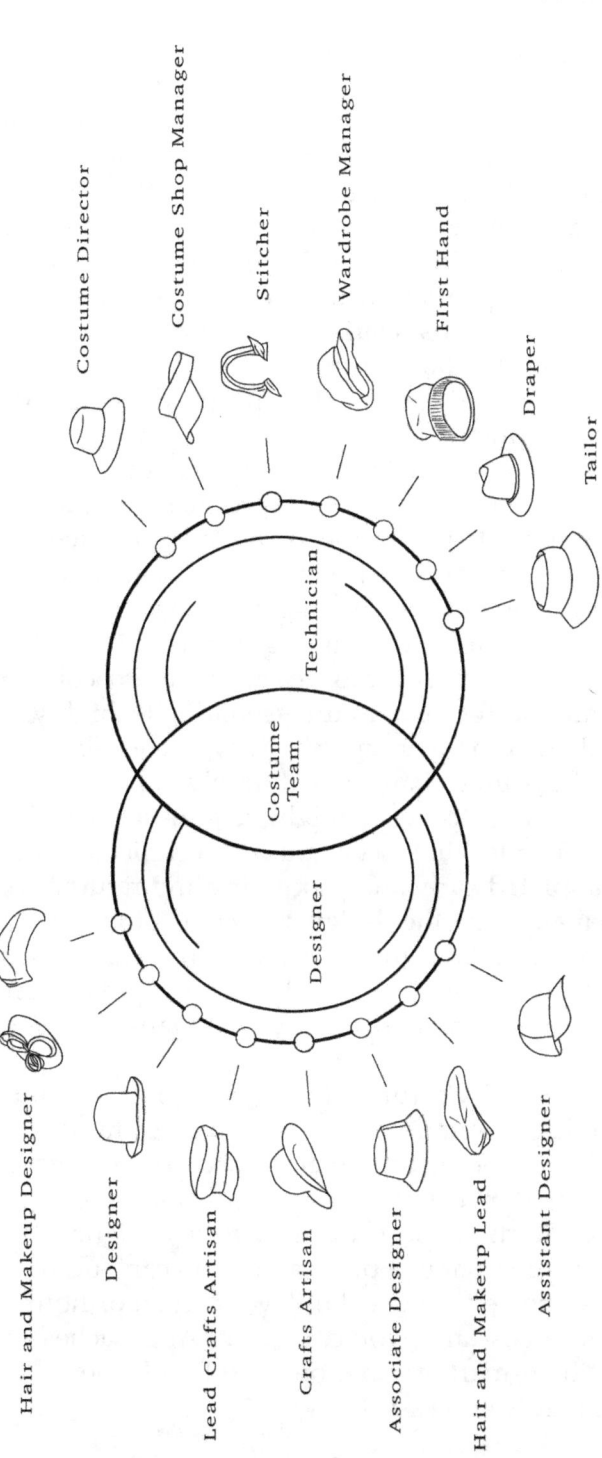

FIGURE 3.2 Self Managed Costume Team Hats.

construct the realization of the design while wardrobe is responsible for the run of the production including interfacing with performers and maintaining design vision and integrity of costumes.

Costume designers are active participants in the realization process making many design choices through purchasing and fitting processes regardless of the type of team. In a self-managed team, the involvement during the realization will require larger amounts of time and energy than with larger support teams. Scheduling and approach to the realization process can aide all team members in managing the daily output required to realize a production with a self-managed team so that this production balances well with other commitments.

Remembering each production is a new creation allows team members to contribute differently to each production which many artists find invigorating. For example, a modern production that can be purchased is unlikely to need extensive construction support but might require a great deal of sourcing, purchasing, processing, and returns. In this case, a technician might step in to facilitate a percentage of this work leaving the designer free to collaborate with the director and performers. In this scenario, it's highly likely that wardrobe will need to be brought in early to contribute to the problem-solving of costume changes that involve off the rack garments. Conversely, a high concept might require a great deal of draping support from a technician or multiple technicians but purchasing can be completed early and processing and returns will be extremely minimal allowing the designer to contribute conceptual detail technical work. Similarly, involving wardrobe early will head off a multitude of problems but also allows for a greater understanding of the concept that will need to be maintained during the show run.

Is custom necessary? Costume departments have the luxury of utilizing expanding resources of the e-commerce era. While not every production, concept, or character can be bought, there is a wealth of manufactured or artisan made items available to augment or utilize as base costume work. The ability for a designer/technician team to see the potential in a purchased item can augment the realization process and reduce the skill level and labor hours that a completely custom costume would require. Approaches to the realization that utilize smart foundations and build upon them in unusual ways are highly successful.

> **Self-managed Costume Team Activity**
>
> As introduced in chapter 2, the three-piece suit is a common garment that spans western history and is often utilized by designers. The approach to a three-piece suit through sourcing or construction is predictably budgeted for by utilizing going rates. Assuming we have a self-managed team working under ideal circumstances we'll illustrate an example that utilizes the designer's and technician's skill set equally. Starting with the given of an early 1930s pant, coat, and vest for a male identifying character, and a materials budget of $500–$600, we will imagine the ideal cut is distinctly 1930s (wide leg pant, wide lapel) with a window-pane plaid. The team has culled through stock and come up short. The designer turns to online purchasing but can only find a two-piece suit. After consulting with the technician, the team purchases two of the two-piece suits with the intention of altering the jacket lapel and constructing a vest front from the fabric of the additional suit.
>
> - What tools does the costume designer need?
> - What tools does the technician need?
> - What additional supplies need to be purchased?
> - How much time does it take to cut materials?
> - How much time does it take to construct the vest?
> - What is the approach to modifying the lapels?
> - How much time does it take to construct and attach new lapels?
> - What are "hidden" activities that take time?
> - What are "hidden" costs?
> - How much time and labor are required to make, source, and alter this 1930s three-piece suit?

PROCESS: PRE-PRODUCTION

Collaboration on productions is a journey; while the end goal and deadlines should not and cannot necessarily change, the process by which those goals and deadlines are met can flex to match the style of the team. Working with team members, as opposed to going solo, opens doors for creativity, but the approach to collaboration must be within reason. Over-zealous design, or lack of creative problem solving, will result in burnt-out colleagues and a less than desirable product. A self-managed designer/technician(s) team should consider the defined circumstances of a production and divide the work required to meet those circumstances, playing off each team member's strengths. Technicians are artists in their own right and have much to offer in creative processes beyond the physical skills they possess. Defining the team from this viewpoint helps create a fulfilling creative environment and contributes a great deal to success. For technicians to fully engage in the process of storytelling, it is best practice that they too review source material. Not being able to fully engage in conversations around the story places the technician in a waiting position where each answer must come from the designer, which is not ideal for collaborating within teams. Collaborative conversations that engage the technician and designer alike in storytelling, focused on character and environment creation, help a team understand each member's strengths, interests, and work style. With this foundation, the team can begin to build sustainable schedules, practices, and expectations for a proactive process.

During early design meetings, once a direction for the set and costume designs has been established and you have started to understand your team, a conversation that reflects the various hats needed in this production and the size of those hats should be had. This can help focus the designer on designing sustainably as well as prepare each team member for the realization process.

Production schedules and budgets are communicated by the artistic/producing director or a production manager to the designer and technician – by discipline. The team often has the freedom to establish (or negotiate) their own internal deadlines in response to the demands of the production itself. In doing so, they consider rehearsal needs, availability of materials and build space, the tech calendar, and competing priorities both for the company and their own schedules. The processes and infrastructure for these productions vary over a wide swath of types of organizations. It is imperative that not only the "givens" of the play be identified, but that the parameters for production be articulated. Parameters include the nuts and bolts available, as well as the intangibles such as experience levels of the collaborators and team member interests.

Understanding what you are trying to accomplish and who is most suitable for the task, is key to the collaboration. The quantity and the quality of the labor associated with an organization, and therefore the specific project, will have undeniable impact on the ability to produce tactile versions of what has been designed. Planning for the production and installing a contingency prior to commencing build will allow for the best possible collaboration. If the technician is not able to complete the task in the allotted time or to the desired quality, designers may consider themselves the contingency or gap insurance for the organization. However, long-term sustainable work practices need to be evaluated. The importance of project management, for the set and costume designs, cannot be underestimated.

A single play title and production approach leaves room for diverse visual solutions for both the set and costume designs. Each design can hit a different note to advance the storytelling; one element does not need to say "it all" – time, place, season, etc. The self-managed team can show a producer, through visual presentations and budget spreadsheets, that one design approach over another can be more evocative while also being more cost effective. In minimally supported projects, openness to an innovative approach that matches the scale of support leads to successful collaborations and impactful productions. Utilizing a concept to address constraints of budgets and/or appropriate labor fosters creative problem-solving and produces content that is new, fresh, and driven by the creative team. Reduced resources do not mean conceptual work is an impossibility. Concepts are synonymous with theatrical design. In working through a concept with the director, the concept will inform the process of realizing the production. Let's imagine a director's concept that sets a production in 1700s America will dictate to the costume designer that the costumes will be primarily rented with the possibility of purchasing available historical basics and depending on the scale and skills of the technician the construction of a few prioritized garments. Similarly, this design concept dictates to the scenic designer that the stage space will be filled by those costumes so with minimal resources visual impact can be achieved more simply with pieces that serve both story and constraints of space driven by concept. In this example, the concept has assisted the set designer in keeping the design to the scale of resources but challenged the costume designer to find a design voice through the rental of period garments that can be difficult to find and/or afford the rental fee. Make the choices purposeful so to the ways the resources both within and across departments can be assigned are clear.

PROCESS: ACTUALIZATION

Actualization processes require working within parameters. Without fully equipped and staffed shops, and therefore without shop heads, the designer and the technician for the project must establish parameters before engaging creatively and communicate these parameters to all levels so that the deliverables expectation is within reality while keeping in mind the final allocation of resources will become clear through the design and rehearsal processes. Parameters that are of specific importance to the self-managed team are the core requirements of the production: compensation and availability of team members; allocation of materials budgets that support the production concept; physical space; and availability of tools.

In all work environments it is important to take into consideration compensation levels relative to workloads. This can be difficult to achieve in artistic environments but ignoring the concept will lead progressively to burn-out. On a self-managed team there may be little understanding of the flow of a season and no natural parameters to scale your workload. When we think of compensation for the self-managed team, it is important to note that compensation extends beyond monetary compensation. In productions of this nature, expanding a portfolio, making new connections, artistic fulfillment, and many other forms of compensation may compel a team member to make decisions about their contribution to the production. It is important each team member considers their own compensation within the framework of the production and has agency to make decisions that reflect that reality. Communicating and working together to establish and understand the team's collective parameters will help the team navigate achieving team and personal goals while respecting each team member's parameters.

To complement the team, consider an organization's untapped resources. Theatres have loyal audiences and often have dedicated volunteers and/or eager to learn young patrons. Seek out these passionate helpers and learn what they are capable of and interested in. All production departments have tasks that must be done but do not require an advanced skill set only a willingness. For example, base painting, labeling, organizing, trucking (picking up supplies, bringing items from storage, etc.). Making lists of these tasks and taking a few minutes to engage with volunteers may save your energy for the work your expertise is necessary to complete.

However, anyone providing an essential service deserves to be compensated. There is a fine line between welcoming volunteers as an appropriate form of community engagement and education, and using volunteers as essential unpaid help.

Pre-determined allocation of budgets can make parameters beneficial or unworkable. Usually, budgets are set in advance of design conceptualization. With the intimate size of a self-managed team, budgets can be negotiated to reflect the reality of the work the entire production team will embark on. In our earlier example of the production set 1700s America, if the producer determined area budgets assuming large, expansive scenery that has now been simplified but the costume area now needs expensive period corsets the production team can seek a reallocation of materials budgets to accommodate the vision. Working across departments is easily done when teams are nimble, and relationships are one on one. The collaboration of the entire production team on this point to best serve production can also ensure that no department has unworkable parameters. Unworkable parameters are a source of conflict. Conflict that arises in one department bleeds into other departments as collaboration between departments is as vital as collaboration within each department.

Utilizing cross-department collaboration can be useful as materials budgets get spent as well. Sourcing is a core competency for production practitioners. For self-managed teams who are typically working within tight financial parameters, it is even more important to be able to source quality at reasonable cost. Lack of quality will lead to the need to reallocate already allocated resources such as labor. No designer, technician, or crew professional can have awareness of all the resources available. But collectively the team has a resource database that should be utilized and possesses the knowledge to effectively research what is not already known. Understanding vendors, return policies, and combinations of terms for internet sourcing is a skill that when effectively utilized can drive the quality of a production up while maintaining a sustainable workload and successful collaborative process. Building relationships with your vendors will lead to better pricing and expanding your network of resources for materials and services. Consider each member of the production and design team an asset and build effective collaborative relationships within and outside of your department.

Proper tracking of the needs empowers the team. A systematic agreed upon way of forecasting the materials and time required to bring designs to fruition will allow close and consistent collaborative discussions between the designer and technician. *If it is not on the spreadsheet, it will not be on the stage.* While build ramps up the tracking of expenditures can be a time-consuming task, which is necessary to respond appropriately to notes from rehearsals, those generated by the team itself, and those in response to the director's and the organization's needs. More accommodations for additions may be possible if a show is tracking underestimate, especially as opening night gets closer. Having a close view of expenditures may allow for interdepartmental support and resource sharing – and in best cases, all desired notes can be accomplished within original parameters.

Revision of the design is a natural and ongoing process as the artistic team assesses their work, and departments come together to combine their efforts. Designers and technicians make adjustments as rehearsals get underway, when actors move to the stage, through dress rehearsals, and during tech week(s). When teams are compact, and budgets are modest, it is easy to go "all in" in order to be ready for tech. The self-managed team members should have a candid conversation about who is holding time, and what budget is being kept on reserve, in order to respond to the needs that come up as the production evolves from concept to opening night. It is easy to run out of steam just trying to get the first idea right, therefore it is necessary to carefully assess the scope and scale of the design concept so that there is time, money and ENERGY to revise as necessary. Expect revisions and plan to be able to handle them. Even in circumstances where plans have been carefully laid out, something is bound to change – an actor has a hard time using the prop, there's an unexpected recasting of a character, or there is just a better idea now that the actors and physical visual elements have integrated under lights and sound.

If the self-managed set and costume teams are small, it is a clear indication that there is limited run crew, and in some cases, there may be only a stage manager. In proposing a design and engineering how it will function, the team should be sure to make work that does not rely on crew that does not exist and to think creatively to accommodate changes dictated by the script. Communication from the outset of the design with the director on the requirements of both set and costume department needs in terms of changes will ensure stage management and performers are available to assist. Rehearsal time prior to tech or at the onset of tech should also be set aside to choreograph changes and train crew members whose primary role is not the crew is essential to a seamless run.

The tech process is the coming together of all elements on stage: from directing down to the last design detail, the form and function of the production will be tested in tech. In semi-professional environments, it is normative for tech time to be limited. On a self-managed team, this process still must be balanced with other commitments of team members and within the schedule put forth by the producer. Because tech time is short, and all departments have significant needs, it cannot be the unveiling of elements but should be a final assessment with minimal revisions. Waiting to showcase work to the director and acting ensemble places a strain on the tech process. In a self-managed team, the team available to attend tech rehearsals and attend to revisions is small. Plan ahead during the pre-production phase and you can avoid the conflict that arises when there simply isn't enough time to properly revise.

PROCESS: THE RUN

Once the show has moved beyond technical rehearsals, the show rests in the hands of stage management, run crew, and wardrobe personnel. These crews are responsible for show run and general maintenance. The stage manager will distribute production reports to communicate notes and if repairs or stocking of consumables are needed. How this impacts design and technician team members should have been discussed and contracted well in advance. It is possible in certain cases additional team members may need to engage. For example, if an understudy needs to be put in or a prop breaks to the point of not being repairable, the designer and technician may need to assist in solving the problem.

Acknowledging the run of a production is important to utilize resources properly. Is it built to last the run? Costume construction suggests a specific process that begins with a set of measurements and ends with hand hems and buttons on a fully lined alterable garment. While this is ideal in a theatrical environment for use in a stock, it is unlikely a sustainable process in self-managed teams.

Finding a balance between this ideal and the $5 t-shirt that will fall apart in the laundry will benefit the entire production. Likewise in scenery, durability must be considered. A chair might have the ideal look, but if you don't take the time to reinforce the chair for the required actions, you will end up putting significant person-hours into maintaining the item. And, without a full-time staff at your disposal, that additional time adds up as you or your teammate make trips to the site – wasting gas money and parking fees or bus/train fare.

The show has a great, successful run and now comes the time for it to close. What happens to all the "stuff" the teams have worked tirelessly selecting, shopping, crafting, building, dyeing, painting, and so on? A strike plan should be developed so each team member's expectations are the same. What goals are needed to restore the venue to preshow condition? Striking soft goods, painting the deck, and things of that nature will vary. Borrowed or stock items need to be returned in their original or better condition ready for you or someone else to use in future production. This may mean late-night trips to the warehouse. Securing access to spaces and vehicles for this step can be challenging, and sometimes overly complicated, so think about this early on. Hopefully, funding for some additional team members has been set aside for the strike, as it is no fun loading a cargo van late at night in an alley by yourself in winter.

CONCLUSION

The ability to work closely in an organization with a small group repeatedly can bring great joy and fulfillment to all involved, but it's not for everyone all the time. Stay within your resources and skills to achieve the best possible outcome for the production and your longevity in the organization.

When self-managed teams are working well together, the production values are informed by, not limited by, the artistic range and technical expertise of its members, who with proper planning operate under the realities of time and money. The self-managed team should have the capacity to be nimble in making choices and quickly determine outcomes. Though many professionals only pass through this level of production, for some these types of organizations are where they choose to spend their career.

Self-managed Team Activity

In this exercise, six people will assume the essential roles of the self-managed set and costume team structures. They will have a working meeting and discuss the givens of a short play, or scene, as well as the givens of their work environment. As they move through discussion point to discussion point, they reveal the scope of what is needed and begin to understand what is possible given the parameters that they have identified. By taking this time, their time moving forward can be better utilized, more so than if the collaborators worked independently and made assumptions about the tasks at hand.

A set designer, costume designer, set technician, and costume technician, set assistant, and wardrobe supervisor have a working meeting. All have read the same short play or scene.

- The set and costume designer come to the table with a list of things the play "can't be done without." It's comprehensive, but leaves room for a number of possible solutions. The set designer might have five "sittables" on their list, while the costume designer might have "1 hat." It is expected that the needs of all characters are accounted for and that the actions are possible given what physical items are listed as essential.
- The team will write a three-sentence concept statement for how the visuals of set and costumes will work together to support the storytelling. With this is mind, the essentials will be put on a list, and they will be discussed by the group. Next to each item, the designer will note an "R" for realistic, or "S" for suggestive. We assume that the director and other collaborators agree with the concept, and that the design approach is approved.
- Creating a set of given circumstances for the work, the six collaborators reveal three actual or aspirant strengths they bring to the table as practitioners.
- The meeting continues as the set and costume technicians take the lead, and the collaborators imagine if the items are from stock, bought, or made.

> It is noted whether stock or bought items will be modified and if they are, to what extent.
> - The lists are formulated into a spreadsheet for sets and costumes, assistants in each department handle this formatting. The set and costume team, independent of one another, imagines how much time for design and how much time for procurement and fabrication is required for each item based on style and source. For design time, think about analysis, research, render/draft; for production time think about locating, planning, executing, installing.
> - Make a list of activities that cost "hidden" time. This should include things such as processing receipts and transporting goods.
> - Tally up how many hours are required of each team based on this rough estimate.
> - As a group decide if this concept is feasible. Considering work hours alone, how many weeks will it take to bring sets and costumes to fruition? What can be modified if the design is not feasible?
>
> Inevitably, the design will evolve from these original instincts of what the production needs, as indeed the crucial research phase has been skipped and other departments have not been considered. However, collectively thinking through a project before a team gets underway with it is a practice that maximizes the productivity of the subsequent hours spent and guides when and where to prioritize efforts in bringing the designs to fruition.

INDUSTRY PERSPECTIVE: AN INTERVIEW WITH COLLABORATORS DANIELLE PRESTON AND BRANDEE MATHIES

Danielle and Brandee collaborated as Costume Designer and Costume Director on *P.Y.G or the Mis-Edumacation of Dorian Belle* at Studio Theatre in Washington, DC.

Brandee Mathies (he/him) has been Studio's Costume Shop Manager since 1994. He has designed *Passover, MotherStruck!*,

This is Our Youth, The Year of Magical Thinking, Stoop Stories, The Rimers of Eldritch, A Number, The Syringa Tree, and *Comic Briefs* for Studio Theatre, as well as *Moth, Contractions, A Beautiful View, Crestfall,* and *Polaroid Stories* for Studio 2ndStage. Other design credits in the DC area include *Satchmo at the Waldorf; Hooded, Or Being Black for Dummies; Blood Knot; Eureka Day; Shame; Vicuña,* and *Inherit the Windbag* at Mosaic Theater Company; *Black Nativity* and *This Bitter Earth* at Theater Alliance; *Anything Goes; Spunk* (Assistant Designer) at Howard University, and The *Wiz* at Duke Ellington School of the Arts. Other credits include *Blues for an Alabama Sky* and *Sunday in the Park with George* (First-hand) at Arena Stage and *Black Nativity* (Assistant Designer) at The Kennedy Center.

Danielle Preston (she/her) is a costume designer based in Washington DC. Recent theatre credits include designs for the Kennedy Center, Lincoln Center, Studio Theatre, Hangar Theatre, Berkshire Theater Group, Theater J, Mosaic Theater Company of DC, Florida Repertory Theatre, and Chicago Opera Theater. Preston has worked as an assistant costume designer in NYC and DC at Playwrights Horizons, Kennedy Center, Arena Stage, Strathmore Center, and Williamstown Theatre Festival. Professional fellowships include Kenan Costume Fellowship for the Kennedy Center for Performing Arts and A.J. Fletcher Opera Institute Fellowship in Costume Design. Preston holds an MFA in Costume Design from the University of North Carolina School of the Arts. Preston is a proud member of United Scenic Artists Local 829.

How was the team assembled?

Brandee Mathies: I have been in residence at Studio Theatre for 25 years.
Danielle Preston: I knew the playwright, who then decided to direct the piece himself, and so I had worked with him previously. I was introduced to Brandee once the process between myself and the director began.

How did you as a team navigate the project? How did you navigate time? What hats did each team member wear?

Danielle Preston: Brandee essentially guided me. He's been doing this longer than I have so I communicated the design and my choices and he knew the resources in DC where we could source from. This was a modern show. The only "hat" I really wore was as designer.

Brandee Mathies: I like to give designers what they want. I have also designed so I am able to understand what a designer wants. I try to put myself in their shoes and understand their intention but also think about what is possible to do. As we are talking, I can mentally break everything down and figure out ok, we can do this or that. I know my resources so it's like have I seen it somewhere? Can we borrow it? Or buy it?

I ask the designer to give me a plot and I start shopping for them. I try to give them a small closet for each person so it's not just one item that they have in a fitting. I try to get them several items they can choose from. From that closet a designer can put looks together.

And if we can't afford what they want, we work together to see how I can create something similar. With Danielle we did that with the men's jewelry.

Danielle Preston: The show was about modern hip hop. I wanted the characters to have jewelry like hip hop artists are wearing but clearly, we couldn't afford that. So, we looked at what designers were selling and recreated it. Brandee was able to make the pieces look really cool by cobbling together less expensive items.

Danielle Preston: I am used to doing everything myself, I don't usually have an assistant. So, with this show, because I was in NYC assisting on another show, I communicated with mood boards so Brandee had an idea of what these people would be styled like, and he just pulled and purchased in that world. We essentially finalized designs in the fittings.

With two characters, the director had this idea that they were going to be wearing matching suits, but they were completely different body types. So trying to figure out how to make them both look good. I wanted a jewel tone purple which seems impossible to find, but Brandee found the perfect suit. Brandee also solved a request right before tech when we had very little money. I trusted Brandee. He's been doing this for a very long time and if I just communicated with him, we could work together to put this onstage.

Brandee Mathies: I try to get in the head of the designer. I communicate about each character and how the designer sees that character: what would they be, who are they, how old, and just a synopsis of their views. And then I can really put that closet or resources together for a designer. So that when we are in tech, the vision is

FIGURE 3.3 *P.Y.G or the Mis-Edumacation of Dorian Belle* at the Studio Theatre (Washington, D.C.); April 2019.
Costume Design: Danielle Preston. Costume Shop Manager: Brandee Mathies

there – there are no major changes that need to happen at that point. We have all experienced shows where there's a whole new concept for a costume during tech. Suddenly the shop is building something totally different in a rush – that's way too late. I also like the director to come into the shop and see things as they are decided that way if there are changes there is time to make them.
Danielle Preston: Our director came in. He was very driven by shoes, and the first shoe purchases he didn't like. So right in that meeting I got on my iPad and we started looking at other choices. In modern shows, you don't always render, so looking at actual items is important to do with the director.

When working with 1–2 collaborating artists specific to your discipline, and when no other full-time staff have been dedicated to these areas, what hard and soft skills are essential to conceiving and realizing the work?

Brandee Mathies: I try to make sure that the designer doesn't have to do anything, or do that much on the show, except be there and not have to worry about anything, especially until we get to tech. So, I'm a one-person shop, it's just me, but I have a background in hair.

I was introduced to tattoos on a show called *Red Speedo* where the guy had a tattoo completely on half his body, with a dragon that literally roamed around his back down into his briefs, and I had to figure that out. We had to find somebody to attach a fake tattoo. I literally just kept calling around a couple places and I found somebody who was interested in theatre and this is what they did on the side, he literally came in and he showed me how to do a fake tattoo with parchment paper.

He showed me how to do a fake tattoo – you draw what you want, on the parchment paper with a sharpie, you take some speed stick deodorant – a very specific gel – you mark it on the person's body and you put you put the paper on image side down, rub it down, and peel it off leaving a tattoo. I had no idea and literally I sat there and watched him do this whole dragon on this guy's back and down to his . . ., but it was amazing.

Danielle Preston: To be adaptable, first, when you learn someone has been doing this for years and you have not, I think you should actively listen to their wisdom and experience. I always want to learn that's why I still assist people. I'm never too old to learn, so in a way, I was assisting Brandee. I was watching him and how his process works. I'm not a costume shop manager, but I appreciate that position so I was learning. For example, he said he got this from this store in DC, and I don't really know DC that well since I just moved here – so maybe in another show that I'm doing I could check out this place. Sometimes when people are designing, they hold their design so close to them.

I also think you have to understand who you are working with. Brandee is the only one in his shop, so understanding his schedule helps. Brandee works really early, which I asked about, so that when I wanted to check in, I would know when I could do that and still respect his time and schedule.

Do you have tips or tricks for managing your workflow or your time when you're working?

Brandee Mathies: I'm an early person. When no one's around I can get a lot accomplished plus I know that I have to go out shopping later in the day, so I want to be at the stores when they open at ten o'clock. We come in at nine o'clock, it will take me till about one o'clock to get out to the stores, and by that time I'm in rush hour traffic, so I can't hit all the stores that I need. When I get there early, I can get done what needs to be done and then be at the stores when they open. It's the same during tech. I come in and get the notes done and then go out. But the notes are done; no one is waiting on costumes: they are there.

I let the designer know this when they arrive for fittings. So hopefully they can consider that schedule and work with me.

Danielle Preston: I am still learning to be honest. I think I've lost a little during the pandemic. Before, I could do five shows at once, and right now I'm doing three and I'm finding it demanding. I keep a calendar and every morning when I wake up, I have my coffee while I look over the calendar. I determine what is happening first and plan that work. For example, today my designs are due to a theatre, but later this week I have fittings for an opera I'm designing. So today the focus is only theatre because that is due. Next, I will focus on opera fittings. I hope to just tick things off the list.

It's a juggling act. You have to find your rhythm with it. This is why having a great collaborative collaborator like Brandee is so key. With a lot of my contracts, I will ask "what are you expecting from me?" Because in some theatres I may also have to handle alterations. When there is a good collaboration, you can trust the collaborator and not have to constantly loop back and babysit the design. That is really hard to do when you are doing multiple shows.

Do you have a cautionary tale for when you've worked with a smaller team?

Danielle Preston: Not really, I try to avoid them. I realize everybody has their own method, and as a guest and in someone's home I try to work within that method. I always like to talk to the costume shop manager early to ask about schedule and how they like to handle things. For example, some shops don't want you pulling things yourself. I try to figure that out and put it in my workflow.

Brandee Mathies: I strive for excellence with every project. I want the designer to have their vision, the actor to look their best, and the quality to be good. I want everyone to leave and say they had a good experience with me and with Studio Theatre. So, I try to bring my experience and connections to every project. Not just when I am constructing something, but in renting or buying things as well.

How can I contribute? Wanting everything to be excellent on every project can lead to burnout so you also have to find a balance and rhythm to the whole season not just one project.

Danielle Preston: I'm a bit of a perfectionist in some senses when it comes to something, so I've had to find a balance for myself. When I first started, I felt like a robot. I got out of school and I was trying to be perfect at everything but that's not really me. There were so many sleepless nights. I remember sleeping with my phone, refreshing my email all the time to see who' emailing me. I've calmed down and I've learned its ok to ask for help. I work with an assistant now. I am learning my limits and my boundaries for myself within this world, and this is something that I'm currently still working on, and I think it is healthy.

4
Functional Team

DEFINITION

A Functional Team is a group of people with common functional expertise working toward shared objectives. By this definition, collaborators on a single production, whose work relates to scenery at any point in the creative process from start to finish, are a functional team. It follows suit that those that work on costumes at any point in a creative process from start to finish are a separate functional team. In the full scope of creating a performative work, one can observe other functional teams – for instance, for a scripted play, the director and designers work collectively to develop a vision for the work – they function to define the artistic direction of a project. Following this logic, we can group any collaborators that work to technically execute designs (regardless of discipline) as a functional team itself. We may narrow the view and look at set and costume managers and technicians as a single functional team, if we acknowledge that they share the common goals of making, finding, and modifying tangible goods to realize the design plans that have been set forth. Members of set and costume functional teams may specifically be expected to actively maintain the production as members of run crews, and there we have it, another functional team emerges. Discussions of production hierarchy do a disservice to the highly collaborative nature of set and costume work. Let's imagine a new method to graphically identify overlapping functional teams to promote interaction between networks, and collaborate to our fullest potential to convey emotion and tell stories through the visuals we create.

Functional teams are prevalent in regional theatre and on festival stages. Educational institutions tend to promote a functional team structure, with student practitioners serving in roles alongside faculty and staff team leaders. Where there is a dedicated scene and costume shop space, functional teams can be found. The size of the functional team may vary but rarely is it smaller than three individuals that are focused on a single objective. As we delve deeper into functional team dynamics, we'll focus on set and costume departments as their own functional entities, and as they relate to each other.

FORM AND FUNCTION

The functional team is comprised of a remote design team and a technical team that has a home base – a shop with a foreperson and/or a technical/costume director. There is dedicated space to make physical items and typical tools of the trade are at hand. Expendables are stocked and the show's budget is the show's budget. A freelance designer can join this team and rest assured that there's expertise in engineering and fabrication on the ground with a process in place to support the creative work and artist. A wise designer will engage in an active back and forth with the resident collaborators to arrive at a design in which the desired look and necessary function can be achieved with the resources of time, expertise, and materials available. In the best scenarios, professionals including carpenters or welders, drapers or tailors, artisans, and painters, are on staff and ready to contribute to realizing the vision. It's a healthy place for an emerging designer to start, especially if the technical staff can be proactive and prompt the designer when more specifics are needed from their design package by asking that certain design decisions be articulated through lists and visuals, when and if insufficient information is provided. This can be a two-way street – where a technical director or costume director early in their career can benefit from receiving great "design packages" from a seasoned designer, thereby learning firsthand best practices of delivering information to a "shop." A producing company should establish functional teams with experience in mind, and support their staff with external resources or apprentices to train future collaborators. Mentorships and apprenticeships are integral to the continued growth in our industry and can be appropriately compensated for opportunities that contribute to immediate and long-range success.

Functional teams are built by producing organizations and scaled to the size and expectations of that organization. Teams can also be scaled within the organization to fit a show slot in the season. For example, many regional theatres have a "second" or smaller stage to produce smaller works. These teams can be formed from the staff but may not comprise the entire staff. A key difference in the functional team is the various levels of management: production management, technical direction/costume direction, and shop forepersons are all in a position to manage workflow and collaboration on varying levels within one production.

Production management will be very involved in the process in the big picture, labor, and fiscal direction of production and organization. Production managers are responsible for hiring all technical staff. Aligning the skills of the staff with the needs of the production season is vital to the success of the entire team and the sustainability and retention of staff within the organization. From full-time, in-house technicians, to show-specific designers and their logistical requirements, to over hire, production management is the position that will have broad insight and impact over the structure of a functional team. It should be noted that hiring is a time-consuming endeavor at any organization but is acutely complex at summer festivals which will utilize hundreds of staff members that are on contracts ranging from full-time to short commitments. The logistics behind contracting, travel, housing, and onboarding are staggering. Only the largest of these summertime organizations will have year-round staff and some of them will even operate and build throughout the winter months. Functional teams at summer festivals bridge the gap between the self-managed team and the functional team in that some of the quick soft skills developed while working on self-managed teams will be necessary for festival functional teams. Unlike regional or educational teams who have time to deepen collaborative processes over time, festival teams have an influx of new team members each season and have to jump into the work without the luxury of developing relationships over time.

Many functional teams will be comprised of specific experts in their area of contribution. As the scale of production grows the need for generalists diminishes and the need for subject matter experts grows. The technical director who also serves as a carpenter, and the wardrobe head who also functions as an assistant designer might be found in small regional theatres, but as the organization grows in size, the scale and complexity of production grows as well, and a staff member's function becomes more specific to singular tasks. Large regional theatres will be staffed by full-time employees who devote their careers to an area of expertise and only wear one hat as a member of the functional team. Large organizations with complex productions require sizeable teams to accomplish the designer's vision. This scale of production is often on the front edge of technical innovation in the performing arts. Many of the practitioners at this scale will have been involved in or one step removed from Broadway productions. Depending on the organization, technical professionals will often be represented by an International Alliance of Theatrical Stage Employees (IATSE) Local while designers will often be union-affiliated as part of United Scenic Artists, Local USA 829, IATSE.

Looking at the production season through the appropriate lens for your organization will help functional teams avoid the most endemic pitfall of producing live entertainment: abusive work schedules. Other pitfalls entrenched in functional teams include a lack of flexibility in the process, delays in communication, and not addressing emerging needs.

A lack of flexibility can become a roadblock to the work within the functional team when any team member is stuck in one way of doing things. Unique artistic visions and unique artists require different kinds of conversations to determine the best path forward to "make" the scenic environment or costumes. Understanding the strengths of your collaborators, and being able to see "this production" within the context of a season's worth of responsibilities for both the home and visiting team members, can guide decision-making, promote empathy, and produce the best result.

Trouble can also arise if any team member is missing information they require to move their task forward – this could be the stock platform inventory from the technical director (TD) or a detail of an architectural element that hasn't been fleshed out enough in a drawing. No team members should sit idly by – all parties should feel empowered to pose questions that allow the work to move forward. Tone matters, and the more projects you do, the better you will get at asking questions. Be clear about what you need, and allow for the conversation. Framing it as "I would like to start construction on the door unit on Thursday and need more information," is much better than griping, "where's the darn drawing!"

The process of designing and producing scenery and costumes is a developing collaboration. Often, a need will arise mid-process due to designers collaborating with directors, technicians assessing the practicality of the design, or emerging choices in rehearsals.

Producers will often be able to accommodate financial overages tied to materials choices and labor needs, especially when an adequate reserve is held. Posing questions as a team to production management and producers can unearth resources that allow the collaboration to flow without over-taxing staff or minimizing design.

SET TEAM

The set designer will interface with any and all collaborators who steer the overall artistic vision for the performative work, sometimes referred to as the creative team. As the set designer, they are the keepers of what is needed in terms of physical space and tangible objects to complete an environment that meets the unique artistic objectives of a particular production. They must be able to communicate the vision for the set through drawings, models, renderings, and drafts. Their work in preparing the plans can happen at the drafting table, on the computer, and in their studio. To arrive at a concept, they may embark on fact-finding missions to libraries, specific locations, or material supply houses. Ideally, the set designer and technical director are in good communication from the moment the set designer is contracted. The technical director will be able to provide information specific to the venue and the shop space such that the strengths and limitations of the resources can be considered as designs are evolved. Separate heads in paint and props areas mean that the designer has more collaborators to embrace when working in a functional team model. A resident painter can confirm available inventory and tools at the project's disposal, which may inform design direction. The props manager will diligently be working to formulate a props list that can be used to check and balance what the set designer sees as necessary for the production. At the end of the day, the set designers need to describe in great detail the look and function of each and every scenic element, and they must understand and illustrate where to position all scenic elements in the physical space of the venue or site at hand. Communication can take many forms, but plans, sections, and elevations are always integral, and should adhere to industry standard graphic protocols.

Technical collaborators are artists in their own right, but their ability to engineer and craft full-scale items is integral to the success of the production. Someone needs to take charge of the build, and although their title may vary based on the organization, for all intents and purposes they are the technical director. They are keyed into the artistic objectives of the set design, analyze the set designer's plan for feasibility, and lay out the build drawings, engineer units, resource materials, and price out the show. We'll assume the scene shop has a manager that oversees safety, tool upkeep, stocks expendables, and has an eye on the schedule from a season standpoint. The TD or foreperson might also build and or craft elements that require their skillset, and when projects are manageable in scope.

For larger producing organizations the functional set team can be quite large – encompassing the paint and properties department, in addition to multiple carpenters. The relationship between the scale of production and the specialization of collaborators is direct. While previous scale projects may have one or few makers the set team will have a deep bench of artisans that have honed specific portions of their skill sets. For example, a large scene shop may have dedicated carpenters, painters, welders, riggers, automation techs, CNC operators, prop painters, prop carpenters, and other specialists which would fall to umbrella positions in other types of teams. Equally important, once the show moves from the shop to the stage, is the team that falls under technical direction but is separate from those who create the sets. This area has a multitude of titles that fall under stage operations and may include: run crew, stage hands, grips, stage carpenters, stage crew, etc. At surface level these technicians seem to need the same abilities as those in the shop however many technicians may be excellent backstage but less skilled in the shop and vice versa. Some technicians prefer running shows while other prefer shop work.

The intricacies of staffing will be very organization dependent, and teams will have sub areas which may be teams unto themselves. Paint and props may fall under the leadership of the technical director or may report directly to production management. The workflow between all of these areas stems from the designers' and directors' vision for the show with specifics of who does what and how left to the organization itself. It is often difficult for designers to know what will be covered by props versus carpentry; the easy answer is, it depends.

Within reason, a set designer's understanding of construction practices should not be a limiting factor to the design. Knowledge of standard material sizes and what tools are required to work with what materials, and how the shop is stocked, are all healthy awarenesses for a designer to have, and can get the conversation with the

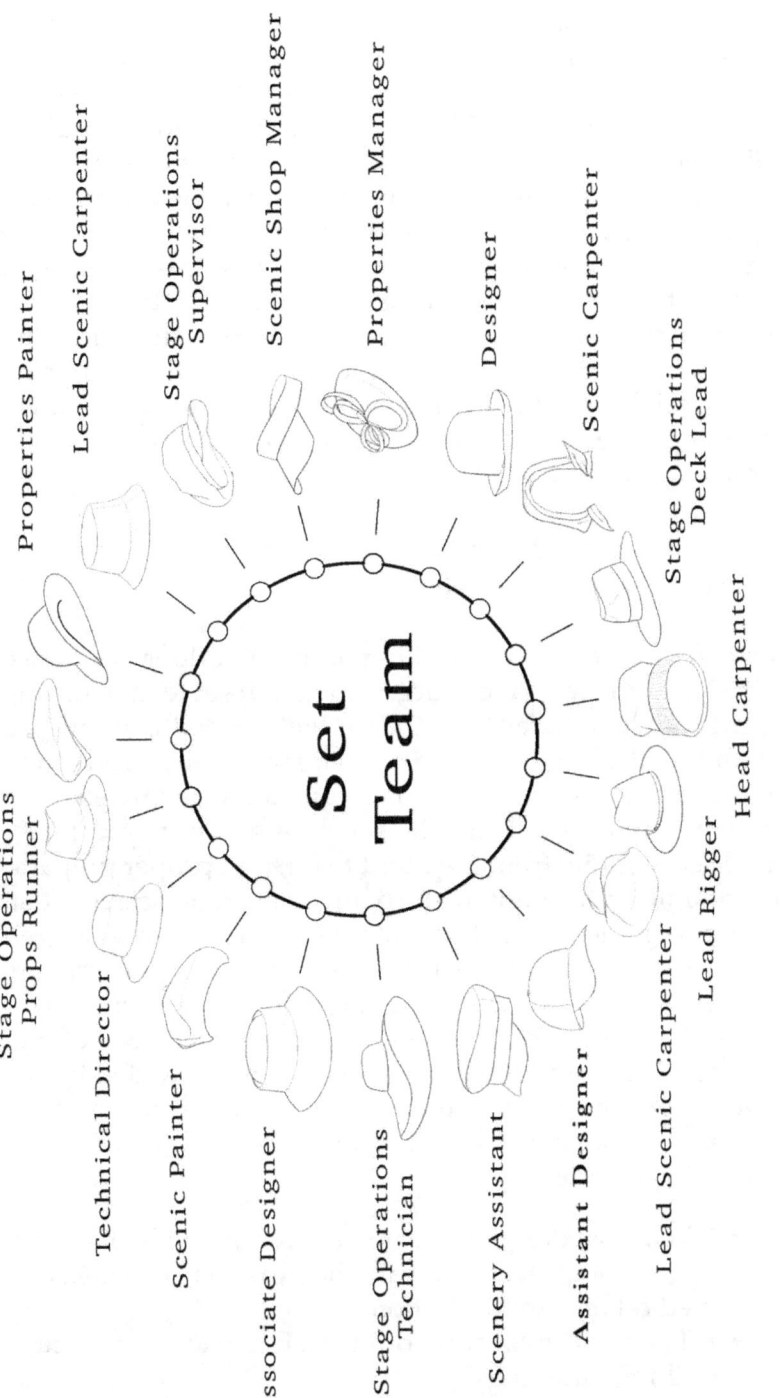

FIGURE 4.1 Functional Set Team Hats.

TD ahead of the game. If a set designer has proposed a design that is impossible to engineer and the artistic collaborators have fallen in love with it, this sets up a contentious relationship between the creative team and the shop. The goal is to keep exploring and revising collectively and be ready with plans when the materials need to be acquired and/or ordered in time for the making to commence.

"Jobbing out" any aspect of a build is always a possibility, especially if the "jobbed out" tool or expertise best achieves the design objective and/or can bring a project in on time. "Jobbing out" is a practice that can be utilized by any configuration of team and entails hiring out a certain element to an individual or business that specializes in the work needing to be accomplished. These possibilities can be illustrated at a "price out," a spreadsheet with a budget line, used for discussion.

Functional Set Team Activity

Let's explore the realistic-looking hardwood floor need once again. This time we have a large functional set team working under ideal circumstances – the budget needed is provided, and all but the set designer is on staff with the production organization. The success of the functional team relies on clear communication from the set designer, timely completion of scenic units from the build team, and proper preparation and follow-through by the paint charge and scenic artist. Starting with the given of the 16' x 12' platform stage, legged to eight inches, the TD will engineer the platform, prepare build drawings, procure materials, and the carpenter will execute the build. The charge scenic artist will work alongside a scenic artist to recreate the rendering provided by the set designer. The show runs for four weeks, and a pristine look needs to be maintained throughout the run. Questions to consider include:

- Did the set designer create their rendering by hand or on the computer? What are the pros and cons of each method of communication?
- What tools or software did the TD use to create their building drawings?

- For fabrication alone, what materials, including expendables, are required?
- Is fabrication a one-person job?
- How much paint did the paint charge order?
- Where does the platform get painted?
- How many weeks are actors on the stage?
- What are the "hidden" activities, for each individual, that takes time?
- What are the "hidden" costs?
- How much time and labor are required, from each individual, to make this platform stage with realistic hardwood treatment?

Following review of the above questions, determine the following:

- optimal size and composition of a functional team required to realize this design
- number of days or weeks from conception to realization to complete the floor
- labor budget required for the design
- materials budget required for the design

COSTUME TEAM

The functional costume team is comprised of three overlapping teams whose collaborative contributions happen in rolling phases. The work starts with the design team. Design teams comprise a designer and an assistant at minimum with the potential to include an associate or multiple assistants depending on the scale of the organization and production. Designers and assistants should have complementary skills. The designer still sets the aesthetic for the design with assistants contributing to that aesthetic throughout the process. The relationship between a designer and assistant sets the work for each role. Often, assistants are offsetting sourcing, shopping, and paperwork but can also play vital roles in the fitting process. The design team is typically brought in from out of town for the production. Costume design teams will be contacted for dates onsite that correspond to fittings and the tech period. Because of the need to be present for fittings, costume designers are often onsite far more than their counterparts in other areas of design. As a designer, the periods where you are onsite are vital for connecting to the entire team: director/choreographer, performers, and technicians. Attending rehearsals, chatting through design choices, and bringing the director/choreographer into the costume shop to see the show's progress both engages all players in the collaborative nature of the work and heads off potential problems down the line. Similarly, engaging with performers fully during fittings helps the team create the character as well as understand the functional needs of the costume.

Connecting with technicians and the costume director/shop manager should be a given much in the way that connecting with a director should be. However, this collaboration is less often apparent. Although the work begins with the design team, it is important to bring in the costume director early on in the design phase. The costume director or costume shop manager will manage the workflow and communicate to all costume team members to build and maintain the costumes. They have a full understanding of the workflow and will assign draping and craft teams to reflect that flow. Draping teams are fairly standardized in functional costume shops to include a draper/tailor, first-hand(s), and stitcher(s). Draping and tailoring are not interchangeable roles but are specific to the type of garment being constructed and are two different skill sets. Drapers and tailors are responsible for patterning, determining construction techniques, and fitting the costume. First-hands assist the draper or tailor primarily through cutting but may also be asked to contribute to patterning or stitching. Stitchers assemble and finish the garment. Crafts teams are not as clear cut and are comprised of a variety of skilled artisans who can lend expertise in among others: millinery, painting, dying, sculpture, metalwork, and cobbling. Crafts teams work very closely with design teams to determine finishes and address the functionality of craft items. Crafts are often non-standard items that require a flexible process starting with research and development and concluding in small modifications during tech once the performer has utilized the piece in show conditions.

The wardrobe team is the final area to be involved in the costume team. The wardrobe team consists of a wardrobe head or leader who will oversee the functions of the department: assigning dressers, finalizing dressing tracks, scheduling maintenance,

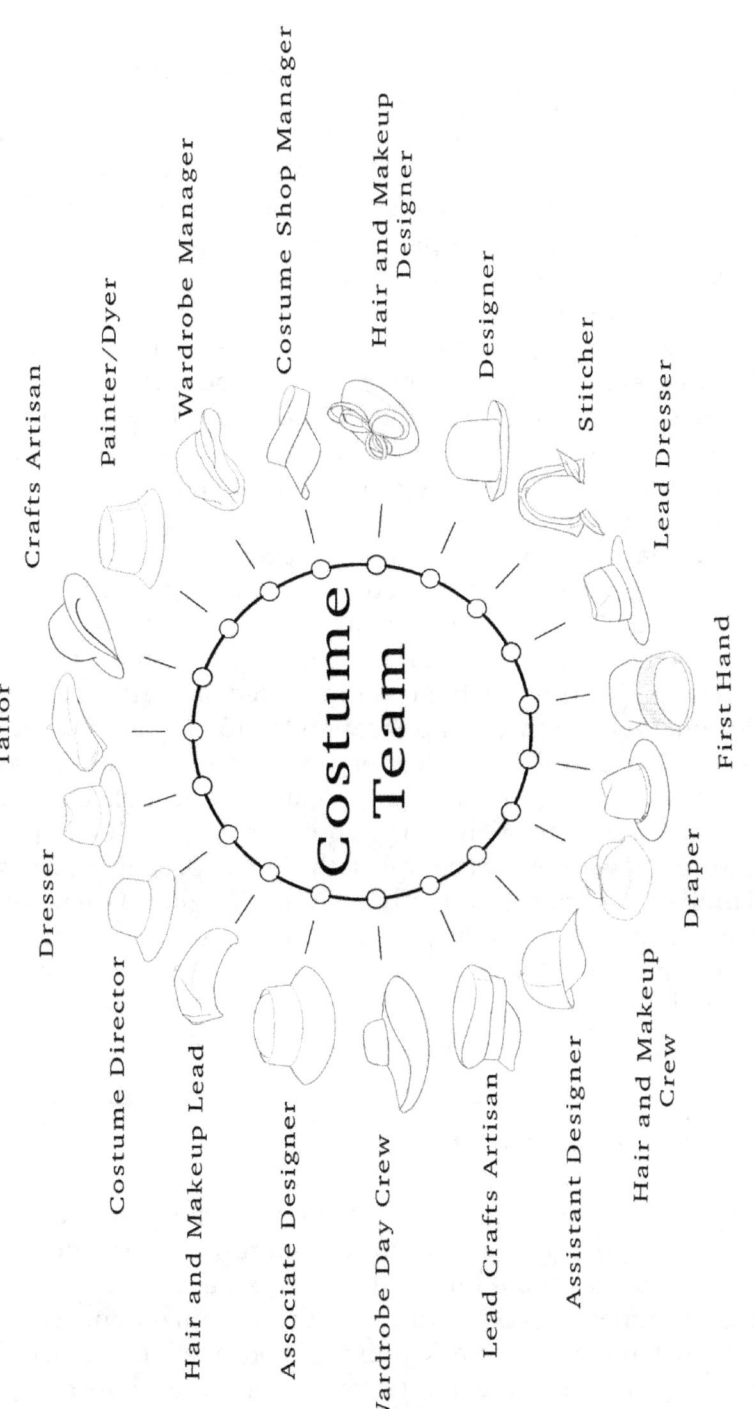

FIGURE 4.2 Functional Costume Team Hats.

ordering supplies, etc. The relationship between designer and wardrobe head contributes to a successful dress rehearsal process and run. Communication both verbal and in paperwork to clarify costume pieces and changes facilitates this success. The wardrobe team consists of dressers and a day crew. Dressers can be divided further into star dressers and dressers. The star dresser(s) will follow the track for the lead of the production while dressers will follow a track that addresses the needs of the production and will dress multiple actors depending on those needs. Dressing a show is an active role requiring attention to detail, the ability to remain calm, and interpersonal skills to interface with performers. Wardrobe day crews are responsible for the maintenance of the costumes. Day crew sizes will vary greatly from organization to organization but generally, they are separate from the staff in the shop who have moved on to the next production.

You may have noticed that unlike in previous chapters, hair and makeup have not been addressed as part of the costume team. In functional teams, hair and makeup are parallel teams to the costume team. Depending on the scale of the organization, hair and makeup may still fall under the costume director's management but the design, fabrication, and application fall to hair and makeup professionals. A wig designer (whether onsite or jobbed-in) or stylist will work with the costume design team to establish the hair design for each performer and then communicate with the performer the pre-show prep to accomplish the look. Specialty makeup design will likely fall to the hair and makeup designer while more standard makeup will fall to the performer with guidance from the costume design team. Unless makeup is extensive, it is unlikely a schematic will be produced. In the case of extensive makeup, the application will need to be done by trained professionals.

> **Functional Costume Team Activity**
>
> Let's explore the three-piece suit need once again. This time we have a large functional costume team working under ideal circumstances – the budget is provided and all but the costume designer are on staff with the organization. The project will have a four week build period available. Starting with the given of an early 1930s pant, coat, and vest for

a male-identifying character, we will imagine the ideal cut is distinctly 1930s (wide leg pant, wide lapel) with a windowpane plaid. The costume designer will make decisions on the look of the suit and source the fabric, the tailor will draft the pattern and fit the suit, the first-hand will cut the garment, and the stitcher will assemble the suit. Questions to consider include:

- What information does the costume designer need to provide in their renderings and paperwork?
- What is the source and cost of the fabric?
- How much time does it take to pattern the suit?
- How much time does it take to complete a mock-up?
- How much time will be allocated to pattern adjustments?
- How much time will it take to cut the suit?
- How much time will it take to construct the suit?
- How much time is allotted to finishing work?
- What is the fitting schedule?
- What are the "hidden" activities that take time?
- What are the "hidden" costs?

Following review of the above questions, determine the following:

- optimal size and composition of a functional team required to realize this design
- number of days or weeks from conception to realization to complete the 1930s three-piece suit
- labor budget required for the design
- materials budget required for the design

PROCESS: PRE-PRODUCTION

The pre-production process in scenery and costumes begins when each designer is contracted. Designers may or may not be contracted at the same time. Often the scenic designer begins their work in advance of the costume design for no other reason than scale of the elements. In fact, all designers building up concepts at the same pace can lead to a stronger outcome as it can be determined what elements take the lead in communicating different aspects of story to an audience. Design meetings are not formalized, but rather it is up to the individual designers and the director to set up conceptual conversations well in advance of deadlines. As a reminder, all designers and usually the director are not housed within the theatre. Therefore, modes of collaboration that rely heavily on virtual spaces are intrinsic to the functional team. The collaborative process during pre-production is often thought to focus on the collaboration between the designer and director, but welcoming the technical staff into a key conversation so that any concerns about feasibility can be discussed early on, can better the process.

When we speak about collaboration in the theatre, much focus is given to how the designer can come up with a concept that is approved by a director. In practice, it is apparent that the designer and technical or costume director need a parallel process where the "how" of the design is explored alongside the "what." In a functional team model, those who "make it" are generally part of the home team, and it is the job of the away team, the designers, to learn how best to work within the home system. The designer should bounce between the creative team and the fabricators until the design vision serves the aesthetic and functional needs of the production while being achievable within the shop resources available. Revision of a concept is time-consuming work and all collaborators should try to stay ahead of deadlines so that the updating plans does not cause a ripple-effect of delays throughout the entire production process.

Producing work as a functional team typically means roles are well-defined. As the designer, a guest in the home of the technical team, it is necessary to prioritize learning and understanding the system in which you will work. This is most critical in pre-production but as the show progresses readdressing and being open to collaborators and processes is vital to the team's success. There will be collaborators you work more directly with and those you seldom engage with. Drawing upon soft skills: respect, communication, emotional intelligence, dependability, transparency, and critical thinking, creates an opportunity for relationship building across the team you have joined. In a functional team the dynamics of the technical team, who likely have worked together for years, can be tricky to navigate. Leaning into soft skills will be required to have a positive experience. When the functional tech team is large, some assume this is an indication that more is expected in terms of design scope. Large functional teams can make the integration of advanced technologies, such as automation, possible. However, prioritizing detail or the integration of advanced technologies is a good point of discussion. More people do not necessarily imply more is possible – find the right scope that achieves artistic objectives, is safe and functional, can be accomplished in the time available with an appropriate level of finish, and lives up to the expectations of the producing organization and their audience. Understanding a collaborator's skill set is an asset to the creation of original work but figuring out a collaborator's strengths can be tricky in the functional team model. An aptitude for soft skills will typically be quickly apparent. Designers are not responsible for investigating the hard skills of the technical team. This should have been done by management (Production or Technical) at hiring and on an ongoing basis. Trust the manager you are interfacing with to accurately determine workloads and skillsets of their team. If or when issues arise, draw upon your soft skills and express your concerns to the technician directly and then the manager. If issues are not being resolved, production management should be alerted. Catastrophic delays or difficulties such as scenic elements or costumes not being usable at first tech should be discussed with the director as soon as possible. Most collaborators are reasonable but last-minute surprises are stress inducing and can lead to less than desirable responses.

PROCESS: ACTUALIZATION (BUILD/TECH)

When the team is larger, organizing the essential documents that illustrate and explain end goals becomes much more important – enter cloud collaboration. Considerations include cost and establishment/maintenance of the system.

- Do the team members all have monthly subscriptions or is there a free web-based tool, such as google drive, that gives access to all without added costs for the individual?
- Who will establish the structure of the drive? Who will set up the drive and invite functional team members to it?
- Will a sub-folder structure be agreed upon and all files must be named clearly to avoid instances of the wrong plan being followed?

The cloud has made long-distance collaborations much more manageable, but as the designs come to fruition, hard copy plans and renderings are required, and a designer needs to be responsible for ensuring their work prints in scale, and that colored printouts represent true to their intentions.

In the scene and costume shops respectively, there are to be project leads who manage the responsibilities of each technician towards the build. This can range from sourcing and buying, to fabricating in any number of ways. The best practice for "in-house" workflow will depend on the physical and personnel resources of the shop. Physical separation of the paint space from carpentry is needed at this scale as is a separate craft from costume shop. As a show moves through the shop a repeatable workflow is developed that maps out the process from planning how raw material, i.e., fabric or wood, is procured, processed, assembled, and a resultant finished good is made. The more a team has worked together, as with a long-standing in-house team, the better they know each other's strengths and can utilize them for the good of the project.

In functional teams the shop will be working within a season so multiple projects will be in the pipeline at different stages of completion. It is useful to utilize a Gantt chart to track linear process of milestones along the process of a show from concept through strike. Thinking of projects in this way will allow team members to hold each other accountable for deadlines and limits the workload of inputting milestones show to show once your process is defined.

Since this scale of production has multiple well-defined departments, the functional team has the ability to collaborate across departments and leverage the expertise of other areas. When scenery has specific fabric or patterning needs, costumes can help. When costumes has mechanical integration into a garment scenery can assist. Expert creators working towards the goal of a show is what makes functional teams functional.

Moving from the shop into the theatre can be a huge undertaking. Everything is tied to budget, how much does 15 minutes of load in cost? The functional team will be able to prioritize tasks that can happen before moving into the theatre space. At this scale, with resources, it may be possible that some collaborators will elect to have a representative at tech so they can report to the shop lead the needs and discoveries of tech while allowing the representative a reasonable day to day turnaround (sleep). For example, if the scene shop works from 7am until 4pm and tech runs until midnight the ATD can report priorities so the TD can lead the notes session all morning with the ATD returning in time for the rehearsals in the afternoon. This could be mimicked by the costume shop with proper planning.

The technical rehearsal process at the functional team scale will fall into established practices of the organization. If union contracts are in place, the schedule will be driven by the terms set forth by the various collective bargaining agreements (CBAs). The time and processes needed during an organization's tech should be firmly scheduled in advance to the point where collaborators will have time agreed upon at contract. During the tech process, any aspect of the show that evolves might require "your element" to respond and evolve as well. As most members of the functional team may also be underway with the next production, the scope and scale of the notes possible should not be assumed. Tech may be the time when the designer is completely focused on the show at hand – they are away from their studio and watching the stage. Keeping a focus on "needs" over "wants" is a good way to prioritize. Forecasting revisions can be very difficult before technical rehearsals. At this scale of production it may take many conversations and negotiations to complete seemingly simple notes.

During tech, another functional team enters the equation fully: the performers. Costume teams have heavily interacted with performers during fittings asking probative questions to alleviate as many functional issues with the costumes as possible but, during tech as everything is being integrated, notes from performers about the function and maintenance of costumes will need to be addressed. Likewise, scenic teams will have interacted with the performance team, although lightly, in the hope of addressing functional concerns during the build but as the performer interacts with the set and props fully in run conditions, notes are inevitable. The practice of soft skills when interacting with this adjacent team is vital. Tech and dress rehearsals can heighten the excitement for the entire team and emotions may be running high. Remember, a performer is the one who must embody the character, wear the costume, or climb the stairs every night so actively listening to and addressing concerns leads to great performance outcomes. The process by which these notes reach the technicians will vary based on organization but in general, designers should include technicians or management in any conversation with a performer that seems to involve a note.

PROCESS: THE RUN

The production begins to run in preview. Although all members of this team have a broad understanding of their area, each individual has a focus, and having several eyes on the form and function of scenery and costumes during tech makes identifying the notes a more complete process. The set designer may notice that the color of the set needs to deepen for the costumes to pop, the TD hears the scrape from a door, and the scenic notices a touch-up. Likewise, the costume designer may notice the addition of trim to a neckline will draw the audience's eyes to the face while the draper is unhappy with the stitching on the hem, and the craftsperson feels the scale of the necklace could assist the designer's goals. The fewer members from a team at the tech means the representative from the department needs all their "set senses" or "costume senses" firing.

When a functional team is in place, it is common to see a run crew in place during a production. The pre-production team and "in production" team are distinct. When there are specialists in all aspects of the set or costume department the execution and maintenance are more achievable, and the work environment should be better. The story and entire production team are properly supported. No one is stretched to solve problems outside of their primary area of expertise. A stagehand or assistant stage manager will manage the deck, if a fly system is in the venue there will be a captain, props crew, and any other hands required for top of show business or scene changes support. Hair and makeup personnel are present nightly, and this doesn't fall to the wardrobe personnel.

Run crews or technicians are an integral part of the team and any show's continued success relies on their attention to detail, skill, and expertise. During tech rehearsals it is important to take the time to allow the crews to learn their run tracks thoroughly. The success of the production relies on it. Designers will be interfacing with this crew but it is helpful to retain pathways of communication that do not cut the technical or costume director out of the equation. Including management provides consistency to process and personnel management.

Key personnel will be required to attend previews which may be scheduled for late nights and long call times. It can be very taxing on all involved especially when collaborators may also be in pre-production for future projects with the producing company or other organizations. Organizational norms will dictate who is on call. Discussions with production management can help alleviate stress on any one position. Once the show reaches previews, the designer may leave an assistant in charge. Typically, in regional theatres at opening, the entire design team will have concluded their contract, leaving the show in the hands of management and run crews.

In functional teams, the strike becomes an important conclusion to the production. Organizations housing functional technical teams often also house scenic and costume storage. Storage is always a premium in producing organizations, is often offsite, and requires trucking and various other special considerations. Functional teams will often have a specific person that oversees the warehouse space even if it is in addition to other duties such as the scene shop manager or prop manager. Costume storage should have its separate climate-controlled space away from the dust and dirt associated with scenery and hand props. The first step to a successful strike is identifying which pieces will be stored and which will be demolished. This conversation can take many shapes depending on the organization and storage options. If the designer is a visitor on a one-contract show they may have little input on what should be saved, however, if the designer is full time and designs in the organization consistently, they should have input.

CONCLUSION

The larger the team, the more specialized its members will be. When a member of a functional team can focus on a particular part, rather than the whole of the design, the refinement of each part is possible, and excellent craftsmanship can be achieved without straining resources. A good understanding of technical expertise available to the project, paired with an awareness of how much time the individuals can give to the project at hand (and not to work elsewhere in the season), allows the team to envision design solutions that engage the expertise and strengths of the team as a whole.

Functional Team Activity

Envisioned for groups of eight, but can easily be scaled back to groups of four.

A single practitioner could also imagine themselves in all the roles introduced, and use the prompts for a writing exercise.

The activity asks you to assume a role on a functional set or costume team and to imagine what tasks you would take responsibility for in that role, and as a result of any givens in a specific text that you have been assigned.

Tasks are dependent on the phase of process. The phases addressed here include:

- pre-production (conceptualization and assessing feasibility)
- actualization (building, finding, working in tech)
- the run (maintain the show and strike)

Step One: Establish Your Hat!

A set designer, costume designer, technical director, costume director, and a technician from each department (carpenter, scenic artist, props artisan, draper, stitcher, dyer, etc.), and a run crew member from each department (deckhand, fly rail, wardrobe head, dresser) have a working meeting. All have read the same scene from a play.

Step Two: Organize Your Thoughts!

On a spreadsheet, list the following functions as headings: Pre-production, Actualization, and The Run. Each team member will list five tasks under each column that they anticipate are critical for them to execute in service to the project at large. The givens of the text should inform these tasks, so if the task you have articulated can be applied to any work, you have not been specific enough.

Step Three: Get Inquisitive!

On a separate document, articulate a question for each other member of your team to learn about them as a practitioner in the context of the needs of this particular production. Avoid any questions or phrasings that challenge the abilities of another practitioner. The goal is to learn their priorities in collaboration.

Step Four: Exchange

Let the discussion begin – ideally, the team would sit in a circle, alternating departments. Put all collaborators' names in a hat and draw who goes first. The first collaborator will read their tasks listed under pre-production. The person to the right responds by offering a task they can add, and then they share their list. The pattern of sharing and responding continues. After the three categories are discussed, draw two names from the hat. These collaborators will be the note-takers for each department.

Step Five: Challenge Your Findings!

In a rapid-fire brainstorming session, the group can throw out any "must-do" tasks that they think the group missed. What givens in the text were not addressed? What technical necessity did no one claim? The point is to pull from each other's experiences, learn what matters to your collaborators, understand what they consider to be best practices, and drive home there is NOT one right process to make a set or costume design a reality. Each department should add 10 items to their list, setting a time limit of 20 minutes is recommended. These lists should be distributed to the group.

Step Six: Interview Your Collaborators

The group moves on to ask questions of each other, those articulated during the initial thinking part of the session. All collaborators should take their notes.

Step Seven: Reflect

The facilitator of the discussion should ask the group what was learned about how each collaborator in terms of "how they like to work."

Step Eight: Drawing Commonalities

The facilitator leads a discussion about cross-functional teamwork and asks the group where they believe the set and costume departments can have exchanges to maximize artistry and efficiency.

This activity can be a team-building exercise or the foundation for graded reflective writing. The hope is that set and costume teams are encouraged to discuss how best to make together before they discuss getting it done by deadlines.

INDUSTRY PERSPECTIVE: AN INTERVIEW WITH COLLABORATORS LATIANA "LT" GOURZONG AND JIAN JING

Latiana "LT" Gourzong (she/her/hers), is from Ocean Township, NJ and is currently an Assistant Professor Adjunct of Technical Design and Production and Technical Director for David Geffen School of Drama. She received her MFA in Technical Design and Production from DGSD at Yale and BFA in Technical Direction from Mason Gross School of the Arts, Rutgers University. LT has worked in multiple states, east coast, west coast, and midwest, as a Technical Director, Associate/Assistant Technical Director, overhire carpenter, and Sound Designer. Some companies include American Repertory Theater, Guthrie Theater, Center Theatre Group, Williamstown Theatre Festival, the Shakespeare Theatre of New Jersey, Merry-Go-Round Playhouse, Washington and Lee University, Rosebrand East, and ReVision Theater. She has also been involved in USITT since 2012, received the KM Fabrics Technical Production Award in 2019, and is currently the Vice-Commissioner of Mentorship in the Technical Production Commission.

Jian Jung is a New York-based set designer. Her works have been acclaimed as 'innovative,' 'inventive,' 'genius' and 'spectacular' in *The New York Times*, *LA Times*, and *Time Out*. Jung received the Edith Lutyens and Norman Bel Geddes Design Enhancement Award for Aya Ogawa's *Ludic Proxy*, and was nominated for Henry Hewes Design Award for Haruna Lee's *Suicide Forest*. Jung designed *Ocean Filibuste*r in ART (Boston) recently, and her theatre work has been in many NYC theatres including Classic Stage Company, The Kitchen, Bushwick Starr, The Flea, Abrons Arts Center, HERE, Theater Row, ART/NY, and Soho Rep, and internationally in Venezuela, Cuba, Puerto Rico, and Korea. Her opera and musical work has been in Bard Fisher Center, Juilliard School, Long Beach Opera (CA), and Huntington Theater (Boston). Upcoming shows are *The Nosebleed* in LCT3, *Bodies They Ritual* in Wild Project, and *Der Freischutz* in Wolf Trap Opera (VA). Jung received an MFA in Theater Design from New York University, and an MFA in Environmental Design from Ewha Women's University in Korea. She teaches at NYU Tisch Design and Sarah Lawrence College.

Jian and LT collaborated as Scenic Designer and Technical Director on *Ocean Filibuster* by Lisa D'Amour at American Repertory Theatre.

Can you tell us about the hard and soft skills you implemented while wearing your hat?

Latiana "LT" Gourzong: A hard skill is producing a build calendar. Together with my Associate Technical Directors, Kevin and Ross, I work through the build of the show to meet the deadlines within the scope of budget and time. We planned out details of what we were able to build and how we were going to build it.

The soft skills are both show-specific and organizational. For all our shows, we have a design presentation at the top of the build. We have food catered, and the entire team comes to eat. This is a gathering that doesn't produce something tangible but builds a community by giving everybody a sense of team and the details of the project you are beginning. Another community-building activity we have added recently has been stretching every morning as a team. It's a mini-morale thing, and a mixture of soft and hard skills.

In terms of working with the designer, before we went into build, I sent Jian a welcome email identifying everybody in the shop and our hours. We also have a virtual tour of the shop I share. I am trying to open the door for designers to tell me when they are free and more about themselves. So, it's me being like, "hey this is when we work, and it's not like I don't want to talk to you, I just want you to know." Jian was good in that she would let me know her schedule; for example, she would have class on Wednesday. I knew if I needed something that I was not going to get it that day. I started doing this in hopes that it would give designers some agency and they would tell me their schedule because the reality is, I know Jian's not just doing my show. Most designers are doing multiple shows at one time, so knowing the reality of what days they are working on this so we can communicate and plan, is beneficial. Throughout the build I also send out a weekly update with photos and questions; this is where we are at; this is what we built this week. It helps everyone know where we are at, and if there is a note on something that is already complete, then it becomes a big note because it needs to go back on the to-do list.

Jian Jung: For me, there is no boundary between hard and soft skills, they should be open to each other. For example, communication, I can't really tell what the soft skill is and what a hard skill is. I have a two-sided job, like any other designer. At the beginning of the job is the collaboration with the director, and the latter half of the job is collaboration with the TD. I have to really understand the other person; I have to be ready to give my opinion in the collaboration to the entire team whether to the director or TD. It is person-to-person work. So, to do work very well, I need to have good people skills. I think compassion is especially important. Having compassion and understanding the person's needs, building personal trust and relationships is important for both parts of the process.

With LT I was very spoiled because she sent me a report every week, and also sent reports during the week, and sometimes with a video or a photo. I might think, "I need this material and to see a sample," and LT would say, "we ordered a sample for you already and it's on its way to you." And the thing is, while the TD is working so hard for the show, I can't wait to answer a question the day after tomorrow – even if I get an email on Wednesday, my commute and teaching day. I think LT trusted me, and she tried very hard to communicate with me, which in turn made me feel like I needed to communicate with her. We worked very, very well together. Communication and understanding each other and trusting each other, are soft skills that we both used.

When wearing your hat, what types of information do you communicate, and what are your preferred methods for communicating different types of information? Have you had a circumstance where you adjusted how you communicated in a collaborative process to better serve the needs of your collaborators?

LT Gourzong: It's email, and then finding the right times for a zoom meeting. I will usually send out the information to be discussed in the zoom meeting a few days before because there is so much information for the designer to digest, and then Jian can prepare. In the zoom we can screen share, and look at stuff together, and really collaborate. It's mostly a mixture of types of communication, but with Jian, I don't think we did tons of phone calls.

Jian Jung: English is my second language, so if I'm just on the phone call, even if people tell me they don't have any problem understanding me, I feel like I'm missing a word or something like this. Talking to somebody on video, on zoom, makes me more comfortable.

But, when you ask about communication for me, the most important communication between me and the TD is drafting. When I draft, I really consider it a love letter to the TD.

LT Gourzong: Jian's drafting is very good. Usually there is a question that I'm asking for clarity on, or something that is entirely missing, but with Jian it was actually provided. It was an incredibly detailed packet with a lot of notes in it. The conversations we had were more about asking questions about the things that were provided, and not that I don't have enough information to start.

Jian Jung: Drafting is the tool that I use to communicate with the TD, I think "how can I give more information to you; how can I make you read and understand myself as much as possible?" I tell my students all the time drafting is a love letter to TD. They need to understand what you want to do, all the information should be there. You are building trust from this first drafting – so you can respect and trust each other in the process.

Can I say one more thing?

I'm a small Asian woman and TDs are typically older white guys who assume that I don't know how to draft, or know technical things, and they look down on me. In that case my drafting has to be even more perfect, to let them know you need to respect me – I know what I'm doing, I know what you're doing. It's like this: I want to show respect to my TD, but I want the TD to respect me – so it's a love letter and blackmail, at the same time.

How did the physical plant and equipment provided by the organization shape the production outcome?

LT Gourzong: If we didn't have a CNC, we wouldn't been able to do this show. It's a curved and faceted wall, with a top curve. In order to make all of those things happen, having that machine was very, very helpful.

We usually have a split shop between wood and metal. But for this show, we mainly needed wood, so we converted the metal shop to wood until we were done, and then converted it back again.

What parallel processes did you experience or observe as the set or costume teams brought designs to fruition?

LT Gourzong: The budgeting – I was working on the next ART show during this build. The next show is starting at ART, then going to Broadway, then on tour, so we were looking at it from three producing angles. We were also in the middle of a two new building projects, and a co-pro with Company One (to be presented at the Boston public library) that was in budgeting, while this show was in tech.

Jian Jung: I was doing several shows while I was working on this show also. I started to work on this show last summer which was a nice long process. I opened several shows while working on this show.

Was there a particular exchange between designer and technician in this process that you feel is a good example of healthy back and forth that allowed for the project to successfully progress?

Jian Jung: This project was very different from any other project I have done for many reasons. One thing that was complicated was that the lighting designer wanted to build lighting into the set.

In the original design, I had a two-layered wall with LED lights at the bottom so that the set could look like it was floating. The lighting designer was excited by the idea, and he wanted to add vertical lighting using pixel tape that would be built in. I thought it sounded like an awesome idea, so I really listened to him. We met several times in person to collaborate and make it happen.

We budgeted this element six times with different pathways to the final. At the end it was highly successful with the center wall having LED at the bottom and pixel tape vertically. The process was very exhausting because we had to budget it repeatedly and I had to draft it over and over again. But I think we collaborated really well and we really believe that it's a good design.

LT Gourzong: With the many moving parts there are a lot of opinions to be sorted through. It's easy to say what we can't afford, but then we have to sort out what we are going to do. We ended up creating channels for the pixel tape and sliding plexi in front of it. But the plexi was complicated - there were four options that would impact the way it looked when it wasn't lit and when it was. So, there was a lot of back and forth. Once we looked at the options to make sure you couldn't see the diodes, we sent the choices to Jian so she could decide which one was the actual look she wanted it to be.

With that level of complexity in terms of collaboration, what are the keys to success?

LT Gourzong: I think one of the keys is putting timing on every decision. In every email saying we need to know by Wednesday or by Friday because otherwise everybody might assume there is more time to think about it when there isn't. I think if we didn't put a timeline of answer in each of those, it would definitely not have gone as well, because of the realities. We don't need this answer in five minutes, we can think about it over the day – trying to find that balance and giving actual time to think about it, but also being realistic; what needs to happen in order to order the materials the shop needs for it to be made.

Jian Jung: Usually the design part comes before it goes to the shop, but not with this. This made it a lot more complicated, but if we tried to do it before it's built and everybody is engaged, we wouldn't have had the expertise of the shop or the lighting team. The teams

FIGURE 4.3 *Ocean Filibuster* at the American Repetory Theatre.
Set Model Photo Credit Jian Jung

FIGURE 4.4 *Ocean Filibuster* at the American Repetory Theatre.
Theatre and stage during Technical Rehearsal. Photo Credit Latiana "LT" Gourzong

made a mockup of this LED tape structure so we could actually see what it would look like, and the shop could see how it would function. The timeline was very important because I needed time to see, but also make a decision. If I couldn't see what it would look like, I may have made an entirely different design to begin with.

5

Contract Team

DEFINITION

In entertainment, the contract team is a collection of for-profit technical and design organizations or businesses contracted to deliver services and products that interlock to create the visual world of scenic and costume design. These organizations employ teams of people, generally who work on multiple projects at a time, and possess the expertise that is needed in a given production. Among others, contract teams can be comprised of commercial scenic and costume fabrication shops, rigging companies, automation companies, paint companies, craft fabrication shops, industrial services, show operations, and design teams. They are contracted by producers; though the timing of that contracting can vary based on the work each organization is to complete. Contract teams are most often associated with for-profit or high-end producing entities: Broadway, ice shows, circus, arena shows, cruise ships, and a wide range of other live event spectacles who produce work with long engagements or no closing date in mind; they may be resident or touring productions. The contracted teams that contribute to the set or costume team are offsite with no collective gathering, have very clear roles, and are driven by the intersection of creative work and business. Teamwork exists within the contract team. In this chapter we consider the contract team's function as the hat and recognize that within that hat exists a collaborative team where members are assigned specific tasks to accomplish a singular goal. For example, when contracting a rigging company for performer flying (the hat), we understand that to fly a performer that company will utilize several employees who will work under the same hat (the team's function). Contract teams are independent of producing organizations and are for-profit businesses in and of themselves.

Individual members on a contract team have focused responsibilities towards a particular aspect of the total set or costume design packages. To the individual practitioner, this does not mean that the work is any less complex or time-consuming than the multi-faceted collaborators discussed earlier in the book. In fact, a contract team member might be under greater pressure to perform as they are expected to provide expert artistic and technical service, with a great degree of polish, and in a very narrow lane of focus. For the contract team members, there are high expectations for the level of finish and function of their work from the producing organization.

The for-profit nature of producing high-end large-scale entertainment can feel blunt to new artists engaging in the contract team. But, when we look at the positives, this can be the most sustainable theatrical model for the individual artist. Producing creative work with structures in place to support that work values both the work and each contributing artist/technician. Contract teams are comprised of contributors who help make the "hat." The parameters of the work provided under that hat are clear at the outset of the work. Well-defined through a contract, each business puts into place standards, timelines, and deliverables that sync with the project and their business model. As an asset, contract teams tend towards personal sustainability and result in positive collaborative experiences. To ensure a positive collaborative contract teamwork environment, members must understand the business lens of the team and bring a high level of soft-skill competency to the project. In this environment, hard skills are expected to be of high quality, and technical proficiency is a must. If designers or technicians miss deliverable deadlines while on a contract team, there are greater financial ramifications than missing the mark on smaller team projects, due to the fact that there are many more collaborators whose ability to complete their work is compromised.

FORM AND FUNCTION

Designers and technicians who are members of contract teams are seasoned in their understanding and approach to their work. There is typically a difference in the way in which designers and technicians are hired to work on contract teams. Designers can continue to be hired as independent contractors or are hired as a Limited Liability Corporation (LLC), possibly through agency representation or as United Scenic Artists members. If the scope of the project merits associates and/or assistant designers, they may be contracted by the producer on the recommendation of the designer. In certain cases, the producer might contract an established design collective or firm. In being the source for all aesthetic choices related to set or costumes, designers are utilizing an ever-increasing broad range of manual and digital graphic skills to communicate the vision to the contracted shops. Design teams have grown in scope as a result. It is important to note that the design team is a business as well regardless of how it is structured.

Commercial shops and technical businesses generally focus on fabrication and these team members possess skills and use processes developed over the scope of their careers. These shops and businesses are contracted as a business by producers. The technicians that complete the work have full-time positions within these for-profit production companies working on the build of the items used in the production. While technicians and designers may directly collaborate on the work, the scope and guidelines of that work are formulated through project and business managers.

The quality expectation is high when producing as a contract team. Quality can include safety considerations, materials decisions, construction finishes, specialty effects, longevity, engineering, and durability. The form a contract team takes fits the design and needs of a production. For example, a production that requires flying performers will bring in a company that specializes in flying performers whose services will account for all of the considerations necessary to safely achieve and replicate the effect. Bringing in teams that mirror the needs of the production allows all team members to sculpt the world without scrambling for resources.

Businesses in technical theatre production are formed by decades-long relationships and reputation building. When a contract team takes form, producers and designers take into account the needs of the production and their knowledge of vendors who can collaborate on the creation of the production. Producers and designers can work collectively to contract the team members needed. For-profit companies have a deep bench with a wealth of knowledge and skillsets. Technical teams have structures in place to: manage technical design, handle shifts in process, account for safety, create specialty effects, source materials, and handle logistics. Clear communication from design allows each team member to fully contribute to the success of the production.

The shops that comprise the technician side of the contract team are often structured like most businesses: standard 40-hour work week, salary/hourly positions, and over-hire positions. Project managers within shops will work to weave projects together to keep all employed in the shop busy but not overworked. In this way, the technical team members of a contract team are also working on other functional teams simultaneously. The shop structure supports the work that is contracted without the struggle of understaffing or shortages of time. Designers and producers are collaborators. These businesses produce quality work within the timeframe laid out by the production. Trust and communication are key elements to the contract team. It is why designers and shops often tend to work together repeatedly: they have established a language of trust.

As a designer approaching these projects, it is important not to function as a not-for-profit designer or technician in a for-profit world. In the for-profit world, you will be able to contribute your expertise in a focused lane – a designer will only wear the hat of designer. Asking for the support levels you need, understanding those company structures, and maintaining clear pathways for communication are keys to your success in collaborating with for-profit technical theatre companies. Keep in mind this is a for-profit model. Shops have a bottom line that considers their expenses: labor and overhead. Good project managers attempt to keep the workflow busy but within the scope of their regular workweek. Delays in contracting and meeting deadlines for each step of the project can cause costs to increase or a shop to be unavailable before contract but after initial conversations. Stay on your game!

SET TEAM

In the theatre, designers often build relationships with directors who, as they move up in their careers, recommend designers to the producers. Set designers engage associate designers and assistants to handle the scope of large-scale production. The set design studio may be contracted in its entirety or the set designer may serve as a general contractor who engages help for tasks that take place in the studio, as well as in the theatre. Although there are industry standards when it comes to presenting a set design, there is not a single formula to be followed for presentation. Designers often align their mode of presentation to the aesthetic of the design itself. After all, clearly communicating ideas and specifications to other makers is the ultimate goal, and each production is unique. For instance, a sculptural environment with many organic forms may best be described through a large-scale maquette, hand drafts, and painted renderings. Alternatively, it may be that an architectural design, steeped in realism, is best expressed through computer-aided drawings and paint swatches. Associates and assistants may be able to work across many standard mediums while others may specialize. A designer may have long-standing collaborators or may contract help to meet a specific graphical need. Beyond studio graphics, designers and their team will visit shops to assess progress in pre-production, prepare shift diagrams and cue sheets prior to tech, participate in load-ins to the theatre, be accessible to the directors and acting company the first time they take the stage, and monitor the tech process with an eye towards functionality and how all the visual elements are working together. In general, it is at the designer's discretion whether an associate or assistant will be the first point of contact for any of these specific tasks. At the end of the day, final decisions are at the discretion of the designer, and must have the support of the producer.

The scene shop will assemble or have already employed team members with intense specialties. In other scales the specificity of their work will fall to fewer people with greater variety in their skill sets. Some of the job titles may be project managers, technical designers falling into specific areas (rigging designers, mechanical designers, electrical designers, etc.), carpenters, welders, CNC programmers/operators, fiberglass, machinists – this list is not inclusive of every job but representative of the level of specialization some commercial scene shops involved in contract team collaborations can reach. These specialists often will not have a theatre background but contribute highly to the productions though they may not work directly in entertainment venues. These specialists are experts in their area and have spent their careers being focused on one specific area of hard skills.

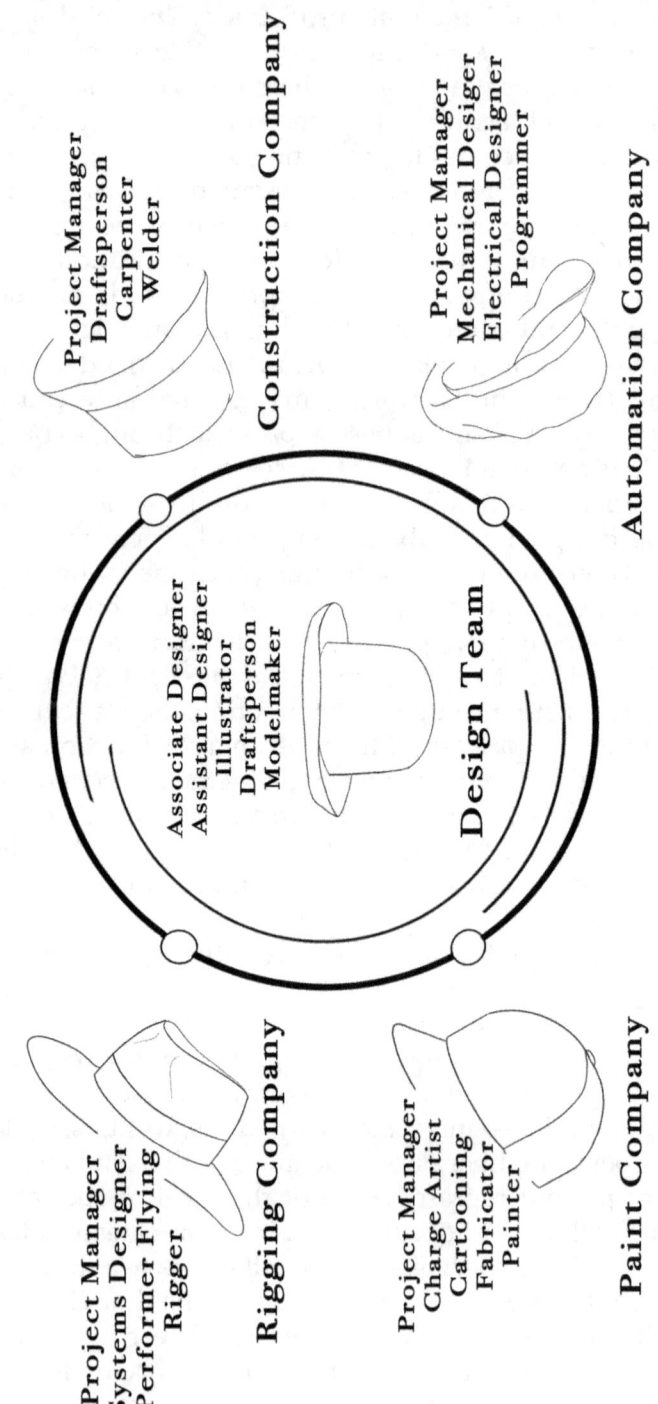

FIGURE 5.1 Contract Set Team Hats.

Some commercial scene shops will have a scenic artist team on staff, others may hire painters as needed, while others may partner with one or more scenic art companies. Scenic art companies range in their abilities and often have space constraints. Many companies that focus specifically on scenic art have foundations in painting backdrops. Increasingly fabric backdrops at this scale of production are being printed as opposed to painted by hand, however those with the ability to create large-scale, hand painted drops are very sought after.

Moving toward the beginning of build, research and development of techniques and technology takes place. For example, is there an automated effect that has customized solutions that may have never been done before? What does the contract specify as to the life cycle and duty cycle of the effect, is there a stipulated test period which must be completed before the effect can be put into the build process? Shop space may need to be dedicated to a long testing interval to comply with contract specifications. This is where art and engineering will often meet and seeking out qualified engineers to add to the contract team becomes necessary.

Contract Set Team Activity

In this activity, the set designer must provide complete details of a wood floor for a touring production. We envision a deck that will travel to black box flexible venues, playing venues that vary in size, 40' x 70' or 50' x 50' rooms. All participants wear the set design hat for researching and rendering the look of the element.

The participants should answer the following questions and add more questions to the list. This can be an imagined scenario or could relate to a script. The modular floor should be able to play in two different configurations and the form and function of the flooring should acknowledge the size of transport.

What questions should the design team ask? (All participants brainstorm, identify additional questions, and draw conclusions.)

- What action takes place on this floor?
- What time period does the design aim to establish?

- Is the floor treatment realistic or stylized?
- Articulate three additional questions.

What paperwork is required of the design team?

- All participants make a list and agree to what type of renderings and schematics are required.
- All participants complete the required paperwork.
- Choose two designs from those submitted to move forward to the bid process.

With each design, determine what teams may be contracted. To determine, list the types of hard specialty skills required to complete the work. Follow up by researching what businesses could complete the various tasks. Put parameters on your research. Decide to work locally or choose a destination city.

- List hard skills required and the businesses that have those skills.
- Compare and contrast what is required based on the designs. Is one design more labor intensive than the other?

Communicate with the businesses to get a sense of hourly rate, flat rate, lead time required, and their expectations for technical communication. Write up a bid for the project; one for each design.

This exercise starts out with all participants working together, and may split into two teams for the bid process.

COSTUME TEAM

The costume contract team can be comprised of the design team, costume shops, craft shops, cobblers, and wardrobe crew. Design teams are comprised of the designer, associate designer(s), and assistant designer(s), and shopper(s). Costume shops, craft shops, and cobblers are for-profit businesses that employ artisans of various skills. Costume shops might have project managers, business managers, shoppers, drapers or patternmakers, painters and dyers, first-hands, and stitchers. The expertise in a costume shop can range from foam characters to tailored period menswear or a shop may specialize in one area. Craft shops also employ artisans: milliners, sculptors, patternmakers, stitchers, painters, and dyers are a few and these shops have their specialties just like costume shops. Cobblers provide services from custom shoes to shoe repair. The wardrobe crew takes over after the work of many on the team is completed. Wardrobe crews consist of crew heads, star dressers, dressers, laundry, and day crew. Wardrobe crews are prepared to both run the production and maintain it.

It is important in building a team that each facet of the design and run of the production be appropriately staffed. In high-end productions, costume teams are separated from hair and makeup teams though they continue to work closely together to create a character. The hair and makeup team should mirror that of the costume team with designers, shops, technicians, and show operations.

The design team in a task team has ample ability to imagine and create characters. Designers can make choices and render exactly what they want to produce on stage without sacrificing to fit within resources. Although there may still be resources to consider, the parameters of these resources are not comparable to any team structures in previous chapters. Designers will want to source fabrics, trims, and be in communication with shops early in the design phases just to have awareness of the availability of these resources. Often design teams who have worked on contract teams prior will have established relationships with shops which eases the process. As a new designer, assistant, or associate, on a contract team for the first time, it's important to start to cultivate relationships with shops.

When embarking on a collaboration with a professional costume shop, it's important to understand the shop's structure and process. Conversations with drapers and artisans should mimic that of a functional team. The sourcing of fabrics may or may not fall to the designer as some shops employ shoppers. All shops will provide, source, and purchase materials that are not decided upon by the designer. Fittings will be facilitated by the design team. If a draper or craftsperson from the shop is completing the fitting, there will be costs associated with that fitting. For costume designers and technicians, the fitting process is a built-in collaborative space within which the teams work together to clarify the creative product. It is important to note the performer plays an essential role in these collaborations though they are not thought of as part of the contract team.

118 Contract Team

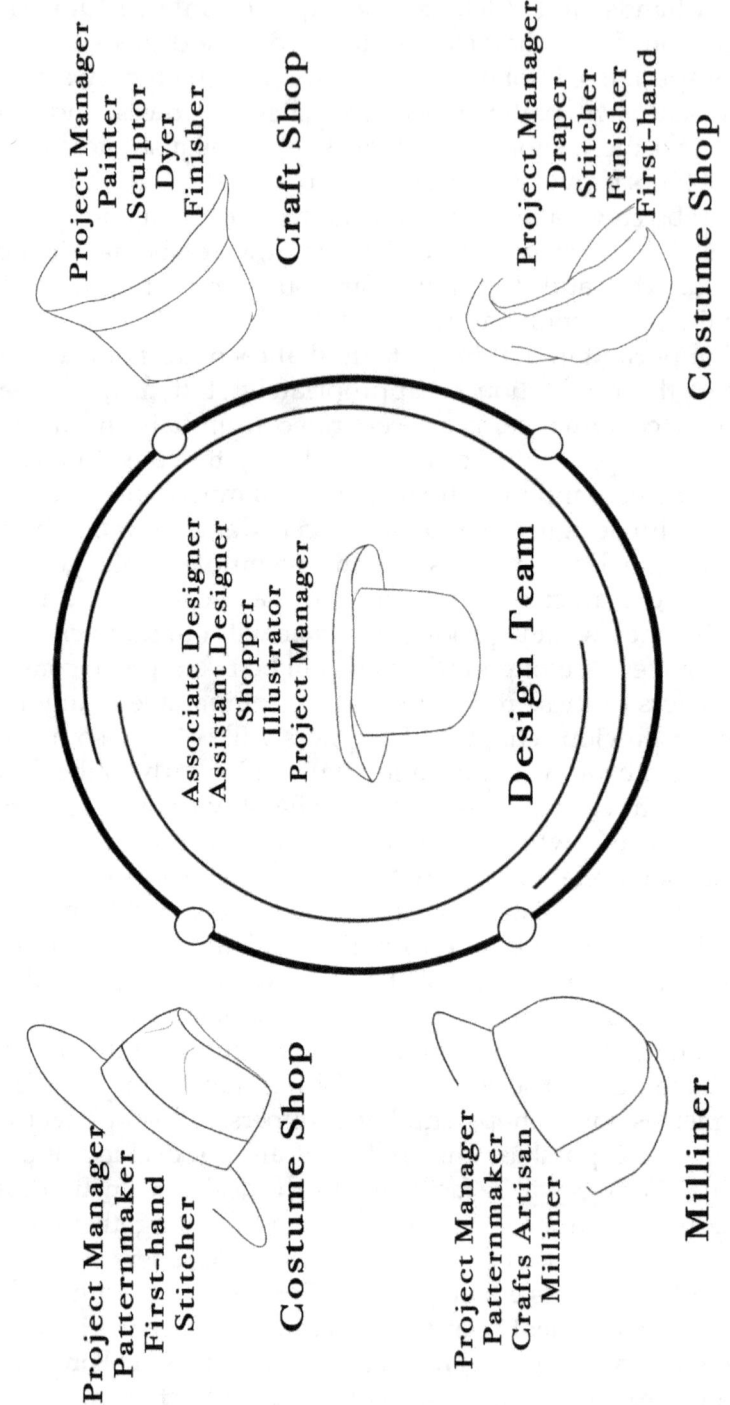

FIGURE 5.2 Contract Costume Team Hats.

Contract Costume Team Activity

Let's return to our analysis of the three-piece suit project. In the task team, we will assume the designer draws exactly the details they are desiring for the character and the technician has all of the skills, time, and resources to realize that design. Starting with the given of an early 1930s pant, coat, and vest for a male-identifying character, we will imagine the ideal cut is distinctly 1930s (wide leg pant, wide lapel) with a windowpane plaid in a size 40L. In this exercise, we will take the three-piece suit through the bid process. Our primary objective is to come up with a realistic bid including labor cost, material cost, timeframe, and services for the designer to take back to producers for approval.

- For each piece being constructed (coat, vest, pant) research and bid the following:
  - yardage
  - labor hours needed
  - labor costs (how much do you plan to pay the tailor, stitcher, or project manager?)
  - any shop supply costs
  - overheads to factor in
- What additional services are needed to complete the project? What is the cost of those services?
- What are the deadlines that need to be met for the successful completion of the project? What happens if the deadlines are not met?

PROCESS: PRE-PRODUCTION

The pre-production process begins with design and culminates in the contracting of the businesses that will comprise the task team for production. The design approach in high-end, for-profit entertainment is a "dream big" scenario. There is little need to limit the design team's creativity at the onset of the work, as the productions are generally well-resourced. Given circumstances such as space or touring considerations provide a framework of parameters. Beyond these considerations, design teams are fairly free to embark openly on creative work. Once creative concepts are laid out and design teams have fleshed out design packages, a fundamental step in the creation of a task team takes place: the bid process. As the design team will not be hands on with realizing the work in full-scale, the design packages in a contract team model must communicate effectively to the technical team. Every single element that will appear on stage as part of the set or costume design must be rendered and/or notated as appropriate.

The bid process requires design teams to pay close attention to the business end of the collaboration. In some cases, companies may be automatically contracted by producing organizations due to standing contractual relationships. But in most cases, production teams will set out gathering bids from expert organizations whose specializations are required. Even within a specialty, businesses have strengths and weaknesses. For example, a construction shop will specialize in specific types of construction: a tailor versus a dressmaker or a metal fabrication shop versus a carpentry shop. From the fabricator's perspective the bid process may start with a request for proposal (RFP). Depending on the exact situation this may come from the design firm or a producer to the commercial shop, the client may also request the RFP from multiple shops. This will be generally what the designer/director/producer has in mind of the production. The RFP will begin to estimate a rough order of magnitude (ROM) which is an initial estimate for the cost of materials and labor, while factoring in profit margins and business overhead, which the organization will need in order to complete the general idea of the production without getting into the level of specific technical designs.

These commercial shops have services they do and do not provide and you will need to bring in another company and scaffold the work; for example, a scenic shop may or may not provide their own automation controls. These details can dictate which shop is right for your design or a portion of your design. It is important to engage in conversations with project managers to fully understand the services and expectations you will be agreeing to when you accept a bid.

Key points to understand:

- What can cause the bill to increase substantially and what will the process need to be on the producing end to approve that increase?

- What is the process should shifts or revisions be needed?
- What services are available during tech rehearsals?
- What, if any, maintenance is available for the long run of the production?
- What is the anticipated workflow?
- Consider what services are necessary and what is icing on the cake: fittings? Dying? Shopping? Support during dress rehearsals?
- How does training of operators occur? What happens if systems fail?
- If the show will be duplicated for multiple markets or tours, can the vendor create many identical deliverables?
- Who owns the assets once they are created?

Once the designer has received multiple bids and cross-referenced these with the budget it may be necessary to return to the producer and negotiate the budget and/or to shift the design to reflect the reality of the bids. During this process, design teams should prioritize and weigh whether some portion of the design should be sent out for additional bids from companies that might provide a lower bid. Lower bids tend to come from new or lesser-known organizations. It is advisable to look across the scope of the design and indicate where it is reasonable to allow a new organization rather than to plug a hole with a design team member. During actualization design teams become extremely busy managing communication and processes through these multiple organizations; wearing multiple hats is not possible given the scope, quality expectation, and contracts. Once bids have been approved by the producer and contracts signed, the production moves into actualization.

PROCESS: ACTUALIZATION

As addressed in pre-production, there are very few parameters for the contract team. What parameters exist are accepted and understood through the contracting and negotiating period. The modes of operating, roles of each collaborator, and deliverables are all clear. There are far fewer negotiating terms of collaboration between collaborators. At this level of production, all collaborators understand the expectation of their contribution and strive to put forward a product that represents their best artistic work.

During the actualization process, the success of the entire task team relies on effective communication and management. The role of the design team during actualization is to balance the needs of multiple companies at once. Design teams must provide timely information so that the process can move forward without delays. Hopefully, the provided renderings and drawings are enough information for a shop that the shop can take over and realize the show without daily communication with the design team. As shops move from contracting to actualization, their built-in processes begin. A for-profit business will have specific processes in place to address each step of the realization process including points of contact with the design team. Throughout the build process, technicians must ask effective and timely questions to understand the scope and details of their project.

Points of clarification for the technician:

- Expectations of use: consider performer movement, quick change, weight-bearing.
- Scene by scene: how does this element fit into the entire show?
- When not onstage are there considerations of space/storage that need to be addressed in construction?
- Is this a "stand-alone" project or does another company need to integrate this element into the show, for example, is a scenic element being built by one company and automated by another?

Revisions can be difficult to manage in a for-profit environment. Scenic and costume shops understand the nature of the work and anticipate revisions to the design throughout the process. For costume teams, these revisions typically become clear during fittings. The designer and technician must engage in conversation with the performer during the fitting to more clearly understand the physical demands of the garment. Costume technicians are well-equipped to propose solutions that balance movement and design throughout the process. Uncovering substantial changes to a garment once it has been delivered will require a renegotiation with a shop and likely an additional fee. There is a point where a revision becomes a re-design and the contracted company may consider this an additional build with an entirely new cost subject to rush charges given the tight timeline required once the production is in tech or previews. The good news is that, unlike other team structures, with the support of the producer, the shop can usually accommodate an additional build and this is not automatically an internal strain on resources.

Between rehearsals and opening nights lies the previews. Broadway-level productions and tours will have previews or invited dress rehearsals, especially for brand new productions. This allows the production team as a whole to gain understanding of how audiences may react to the work that has happened in rehearsals. If all is well, the production will open soon after. Occasionally on large Broadway productions previews will be extended for a variety of reasons including changes to the book, technical challenges, or other issues in the structure of the production.

PROCESS: THE RUN

Productions produced by teams of this nature typically happen in venues that are unionized. Because of this, the contract team shifts. The makers have completed their work and show operations will take over. There can be exceptions to this and/or organizations that hire union specialists who will engage in the tech and run process or if the shop that built the set or costume piece is local there may be an agreement regarding extensive alterations being completed by the original maker. In some scenarios, the product has been shipped and received at a location where the show's crew will take full responsibility for integrating the production during load-ins and the tech process. The tech process itself is typically longer than in other producing entities and is followed by a period of preview performances during which adjustments continue to be made to the set and costumes.

For scenic teams it will generally come down to whether the modification can happen on site with the tools and personnel available or if the revision will need to be pushed through the shop and then delivered to the venue. Will the union stage hands be able to complete this change? Does it require structural welding of aluminum? The scope of the change will impact the timeline, feasibility, and ultimately cost. At the scale of production many of the structural and automated components have gone through an engineering analysis and any deviation from the specification laid out by the engineer will shift liability to the team member who modified the design. This is not a problem until an accident occurs. On a Broadway show the shop is generally at least an hour away or more, sometimes in another time zone. These revisions can be done but are usually very costly for the producers. In the world of commercial building construction these are referred to as change orders and again come with a hefty price.

During the run, it is the responsibility of the wardrobe or crew head to maintain the original design intent through effective management. Once a production of this scale has opened, the work of the design team is complete except in the case of re-casting. Long-running productions periodically see cast members cycle out of the show. Depending on the costume design, a designer or associate may be contracted to design new costumes for the new performer. Or, the wardrobe head will work directly with the original shop to create new costumes if the design can be easily replicated. Costume shops profit more from rebuilds for new performers and duplication of original shows on tours and in new locations. The time-consuming problem-solving of the original version which can require extensive resources now must only be replicated which takes few resources however, the cost of the build remains the same.

On the other hand, static scenery does not require much change or upkeep during even a lengthy run with cast changes, however in all likelihood at this scope of production there are many complicated high detail elements packed into the set. These highly technical effects likely run on some variety of computer control, but regardless of whether windows-based or industrial controlled machines are deployed they will require some version of maintenance, repair, and eventually replacement. It is common for scene shops which manufacture and engineer scenic automation systems to provide inspections, support, and service over the run of the production.

Many contract team productions function as tours. The technicians which run the show will also be responsible for loading it in and out of the various venues the show plays. This part of the team will lead local stage hands in the assembly, run, and disassembly of the show's technical elements. The specialized skills here can expand exponentially to include people like truck drivers, catering, health and safety, security, and fire marshals. While the production may be locked in on opening night there may specific safety or logistic concerns which require ongoing rehearsals such as an aerial rehearsal, quick change rehearsals, fire watch, and automation pre-show checks.

Organizations working with the types of budgets, scales, and exposure that necessitate a contract team will likely store, sell, rent, or reuse the assets that have been created by their initial project. Scenic elements may have come from stock modules that will have further life in other productions. Perhaps the performers are contractually offered their costumes at the end of the tour; this should hopefully be discussed long before the last show. The idea of not being wasteful and hoping to reuse pieces for future productions and creating stock items where possible is a common through line regardless of scale of production.

CONCLUSION

Contract teams may be where many artists aspire to work when they first set out, however there are some sacrifices which are made by those working in these teams. Large-scale productions happen on a global scale and frequent travel may be required, the scale and budgets are large, therefore so is the pressure. Many team members come to work within large teams, with audiences in the millions, by starting on a smaller scale and learning the processes and skills, both hard and soft, which are required to excel on contract teams.

Contract Team Activity

The purpose of this assignment is to recognize the variety of expert artists and technicians that come together to make a single, large-scale production. It asks you to consider commonalities across departments so that practitioners realize they have many outlets for primary research when approaching creative problems. The exercise promotes awareness of the hard skills possessed by designers and technicians and allows for reflection on what department a practitioner might be equipped to function in within or beyond their primary area of expertise.

In this contract teams chapter, each hat represents a contracted studio or shop and the names that are "pulled from the hat" are the team members within that department. For example, the hat can represent the scene painting studio and a position name is scenic charge artist. A facilitator is encouraged to put names of positions in an actual hat. They also select a production photo from a renowned, fully realized dramatic work, and/or a production realized by their organization to share with the group. A participant will draw a name from the hat, and for each position the group will imagine and note:

- What hard skills were required of the person in this position, in the context of this particular production?
- Are these skills applicable to any other hats/positions within the same department and across the production as a whole?

A think/pair/share structure will lead to more imagining and promote collaborative discourse, but certainly a solo practitioner can explore these ideas on their own through reflective writing. Discoveries may be made by the individual about a particular role within a contract team, and an emerging practitioner may seek out a professional in that line of work to learn more about the day-to-day life of someone in that position. If this activity is used for professionalization, one might choose to network by researching who held a position on the particular production explored, and reach out to them directly for additional information regarding their process or to aid in the imagining of the above.

INDUSTRY-PERSPECTIVE: AN INTERVIEW WITH COLLABORATORS JOHN KRISTIANSEN AND BRIAN BLYTHE

John Kristiansen New York, Inc. (JKNY) is a custom costume shop serving the entertainment community by providing high-quality costumes for theatre, dance, film, television, and live-action entertainment. With work that has been seen on Broadway, in regional theatres, national tours, films, stadium events, dance performances, theme parks, and concerts, JKNY works with designers directly; from discussing the first sketch, to choosing fabrics, to hosting fittings in their midtown Manhattan studio. JKNY works to make every designer or client feel supported throughout the construction process, and to deliver garments of uncompromising quality.

In response to the shutdown of the entertainment industry in the wake of the Covid-19 pandemic, JKNY founder, John Kristiansen, and business manager, Brian Blythe, created the Costume Industry Coalition (CIC) to advocate for the survival of the custom costume industry of New York City.

How did you set out to build your business?

John Kristiansen: Well it's always been every shop's goal to do the best work they can, at all times and that's both in quality of product and in quality of price. So when I started for a long time it was my goal, I think it was in my mission statement, to bring a more affordable costume to Broadway and film. But I found out, as we went through our process that the more necessary idea was the most perfect costume. So that changed a lot in the way we approach things because as I was building the affordable thing that people were claiming they wanted, that wasn't what they wanted. They wanted to make sure they didn't have challenges, because you know producers make quite a bit of money-making theater in New York or in movies so there are huge financial implications on the line. My idea of trying to provide something cheap and quick wasn't really what anybody was looking for except possibly some dance companies, but even they were not necessarily on that page. So, then, we pivoted and upgraded. I hired a lot more people; it's not just a one man show like it used to be.

We do a lot of outside of the box things. Ann Hould-Ward described us as "when you want something outside of the box, you go to John Kristiansen's." Which I guess is true. We do the walk around animated clocks for *Beauty and The Beast* in Shanghai, we do LED costumes, costumes made of plastic like the ones in *Six*. It is now my goal to make sure that we do the highest quality, which does come with a price. That people's needs are satisfied, and that the performer can move and function well, and that the costumes or wardrobe evolve – so like a big part of building the ones we're doing for *Six* now, we're finding the washable moments, so that things can come apart and have less wear and tear and then fit back together effortlessly so that people can move and dance.

Can you describe the structure of the business/shop as it stands today?

Brian Blythe: As you know, John is the President who started the company. He's also a draper. When I came in as the business manager, we had 10 employees, now we have about 50. There are three departments: dressmaking, tailoring, and crafts/millinery. We are considered a full-service shop in New York City. There are other shops that are just dressmaking or tailoring or crafts. We can do basically anything that's brought to us. As the business manager I handle everything from human resources to bidding. We have about three and a half project managers who are the hub of information, and the conduit between designers or design teams and our workers so they are constantly compiling information and keeping bibles up to speed. They check in with the makers to see if we are hitting deadlines, scheduling fittings, looking at materials. The maker teams vary on department. Dressmaking teams are a draper, first-hand, stitcher, and finisher. Once the pattern gets handed over to the first-hand it is really the first-hand that is pushing the project through the process. The draper goes on to the next project. In tailoring, that is different. The tailor really stays with the assembly. They have a cutter on the team and will share finishers with the dressmaking teams. In crafts, we have a lead and the team contributes to the projects based on their expertise. Things are a little looser structurally in crafts. The team works together and it is less a process down the line like dressmaking.

FIGURE 5.3 In process at John Kristiansen New York.

How do you book work? What is the process like when beginning a project on a contract?

Brian Blythe: There's quite a number of different ways that the work comes to us. Primarily it's based on relationships. Designers and associates have built relationships over time with particular shops. At JPKNY, there is a shorthand that has developed between John and the designer. Trust has been nurtured there. This trust will lead particular designers to prioritize particular shops to work with them directly. The process always starts with the sketch and the idea from the designer. Typically, we will have a bid session. In the most ideal world we are sitting directly with a designer. It is less ideal to be meeting with an associate who is translating because, as you know, sometimes much can get lost in translation. But, based on schedule or location, sometimes it's necessary to meet only with the associate. I think what is coming out of the pandemic, which is interesting, is zoom. Everyone feels like we can just meet on zoom but it's not as much fun. In the costume world it can be useful to be in person where you are able to flip through tactile resources.

So, the bid process begins with the sketch. "Sketch" is a broad term. We have designers who do what I call the whisper of an idea. Usually these are watercolor and the detail isn't spelled out but the idea is there. Contrast that with the computerized illustration which is very detailed work. There are also corporate clients where you are getting fully fleshed out information; every detail they want right down to pantone colors. So it's a wide range. The importance of the bidding processes is to get out of the designer as much as possible so we can understand their vision and understand what we are actually bidding on. Again, this is where the shorthand of knowing a particular designer is useful to accurate pricing.

John Kristiansen: Once the bid session happens, Brian will set up a sheet for me to go through and figure out all the steps that need to happen in making the costumes. One note on this, that is funny to me, is I don't think designers understand necessarily that the more words that are used to describe the sketches, the more things that I have to be committed to. Which is why I keep telling people, I appreciate the descriptions and that you think that this is what it needs to be, but I can do this, or this, or this to create that. For example, there is printing painting versus hand painting. We can offer all of those thoughts and ideas. Back in the day, it was a much more collaborative process during the bidding process, and now it has become very scripted. People are more committed to what they think they know versus trying something new.

It's a great idea to come through with an idea of collaboration and have a fluid conversation instead of, "here's what I'm telling you to do." We bring a wealth of experience to any project. We have people coming in from foreign countries that do things totally differently, and different backgrounds, and we should be able to gather all of those ideas and skills and the information from the designer and tell you what might work for your project.

Once we go through the bidding process we launch into fabrication meetings. Ideally, that would all take place around the big roundtable. We all sit together and throw swatches around and look at samples, look at old projects that we've done to show what the potential is. We try to make some loose decisions and start making some samples at that point. About a week later we'll bring everybody back together again to see the samples and decide how to move forward. We want to make sure everybody's on the same page so we're not just leaping to the finish line.

Then, we look at muslins on the forms before we move into the fitting process.

As experts in build processes, can you describe your shop's process through fitting and the collaboration with the design team?

John Kristensen: We start with a fitting in muslin and then ideally we have two to three fittings in full fabric. The second fitting is in full fabric with plenty of seam allowance so that everything can be changed as needed. There is only so much we know while a new play is being produced. Much of the information on quick changes or quick rigging are coming out of a rehearsal process so we allow for changes. The third fitting will be more about fit and finish, and then the fourth fitting would be the check fit to just to make sure that everything works and that's time permitting.

Once we are in a fitting process, there is a whole different language because we initiate an actor into the process, who has many, many thoughts on what they are going to do and how they can be assisted by the costume ideally. There are a lot of times I'll end up having sidebars with actors who have thoughts that they want to share and sidebars with designers who also have thoughts to share. So, I'm trying to do my best to try to get everybody on the same page and to make sure that everybody's needs are being met. I have a really crackerjack project manager in the room at all times writing down all the thoughts and feelings that we're going through as this process ensues. That's a big step.

I do my best to listen and respond. I also sometimes just watch the designer interact with the actor and try to do my best to interpret what they're looking for.

There are other conversations that are going on in the other fittings for the show so I try to group the whole experience of the show together. Because sometimes actors go rogue as if they're doing a different show in their own mind. So you have to keep putting the pieces together as you go forward.

And my first-hands, you know they're going to go off the rail when they get the little project to try to get things going, the way they see fit. There were a lot of requests when they were building the costumes for *Six*. We went through three years of working on the same sets of costumes. Gabriella Slade came in with great ideas and we had the prototypes that were made in the UK. She wanted to do an upgrade so there was a lot of conversation about how these would be upgraded. Some requests remained that were taken and run with, but it made the costume really hard and really expensive to make.

When coming back to the startup post pandemic, we were able to talk more about things that were being requested that were a little excessive and bring them back to a place to make sure that the price point is meeting the expectation.

Costumes in general are a ton of collaboration and conversation and navigating all the individual needs. *Six* was also a show where we were able to bring everybody together in the process. Actors on stage, understudies, choreographers, directors, anyone is more than welcome to come to my fitting room to work together in one place where that actor feels safe to say what's on their mind, and I feel safe to say what's on my mind. I bring to the room my drapers, my first-hands, and my crafts people. Everybody has a valuable opinion and thought process. All of that collaboration, and these costumes are Tony award-winning costumes.

Everyone can make this a better process if we include the group into the conversation – it's an amazing place to be. Everybody comes in and is very vulnerable. The actor is literally getting undressed. The fitting room is a place to have conversations about what they're worried about, what they're concerned about, how their day is going – it's just such a personal and private place to relate with one another. It's beautiful.

So you deliver the costumes to Broadway for rehearsals, and there is an issue that comes up. What happens at that point?

Brian Blythe: Once the costumes are delivered to a Broadway show, the wardrobe union takes over and it really is their responsibility to do what is necessary to care for them and get them on stage. This is another type of collaboration. The most successful collaboration with wardrobe is when they get involved early. They are talking to choreographers or directors and bring information during the build process so we understand quick changes or things that need to happen with the costumes. Rigging is usually the biggest issue. We can plan ahead and deliver the costume with the rigging the wardrobe team wants.

This is also something we have talked to Broadway general managers about because they don't understand why they are immediately paying a day rate to change the costume after it has been delivered.

But, if there is a bigger issue with a costume and they need to come back to us we work it out. It's not difficult because we are right there in New York. For example, last season during a preview for a Broadway show, there was suddenly a quick change that wasn't working. The production called a huge rehearsal for it, and requested John be there with the stage manager, actor, wardrobe person – a lot of people.

They had changed the choreographer during previews or rehearsals, and the costume was engineered to be pulled off with a downward sweeping motion from the performer's right shoulder. The changed choreography pulled it straight off her chest. So when John pointed that out, and they shifted back to the original choreography, the dress worked. This exemplifies that people don't understand these costumes are specifically engineered. You have to honor the engineering.

Costume Industry Coalition

John and Brian started the Costume Industry Coalition out of necessity during the Coronavirus Pandemic. CIC unites the New

York City costume businesses to advocate for change throughout the industry.

How did the Costume Industry Coalition (CIC) come together and what is it?

Brian Blythe: March of 2020, John was supposed to go to the opening night of *Six* on Broadway but he went to the hospital instead. By the time he came out of the hospital, the entire industry had shut down. As the timelines for reopening continued to stretch on and on, we literally were in our home in April wondering, are we going to have to sell the business, sell our house, and move to my sister's basement. I saw that Charlotte St. Martin, who is the President of the Broadway League, was joining a task force, an advisory council to the mayor's office, on reopening Broadway and I knew because we weren't union affiliated, there wouldn't be a voice for the shops. So to make sure that she was speaking up on our behalf, I worked on introducing us via email. I reached out to the other shops at the time and said, you know, obviously you're closed; we know that we are sitting ducks right now and we know we employ a workforce and that we need to stay afloat so that we can rehire them when all this is over. Sally Ann Parsons pushed me to not just include the makers, but our subcontractors as well, so our pleaters, printers, embroiderers, painters, dry cleaners, and bra tenders.

We really wanted to make sure that once the lights went back on Broadway, in particular, we were still there, so it really was about trying to figure out how to get through to the end of the pandemic. We started sharing resources – sharing information. When we tallied what we had lost, it was millions in gross revenue. We were millions in collective debt, because the government only did so much. For me connecting with Be An #ArtsHero was really for me a turning point because they were quantifying the economic impact of the creative economy nationally. It really changed my thinking from arts are good for the soul, to the arts are actually good for the economy.

John Kristiansen: Advocating is something that everybody should do. I think the challenge became that back when I was first in New York, I worked at a union shop and at that point, I knew I was making $8 an hour making $40,000 gowns, and I loved my job. I loved everything about it: the shop and the shop owner. I was enamored with it. It was just a wonderful experience, and I, you know, totally drank the Kool-Aid for the industry.

Since then I've learned so much more about how to be a better employer and to make an industry better. As an industry, we've really been falling behind. I was shocked when one of the first things that we had to do was to go through our payroll to get a PPP loan during the pandemic. I hadn't ever looked at my payroll to see how much my employees made. Some of them had worked here for a very long time, without getting any raises or bonuses because they've never asked. We have different languages – they have different backgrounds, and some people just fell through the cracks while some people were very vocal and their pay rates had skyrocketed. So the first thing we did as part of starting our pathway through the pandemic was to go through and look at those issues from the inside. But then it became quite apparent that, if I raise all my pay rates, but the other shops don't raise their pay rates, we're creating a disparity there. Brian and I were talking one night and we thought that maybe it was a good idea to get a few of the shop owners together and just talk through things, and then that led to getting all shops together and that's all levels, so the independent dyers and crafters: everybody. We got together so we could all support one another because, as we all know, the shows are built by many shops and we were all shut down. We just started growing the group together, we would meet every Sunday night to talk about whatever issues were coming up. Brian was doing a lot of advocacy: talking to Congressmen, the Broadway Producers League, and the American Theatre Wing. I think it was Tony Leslie James who called one night to say that what we're doing is great but it really needed somebody to voice it for us. I had just done Cher's tour and I was hanging out with her pre pandemic, so I called them. I asked them to tweet a little bit or do something to promote it, and they ended up getting us in touch with Be An #ArtsHero who were doing a whole grassroots campaign to get a normalization of the funding.

The level of earnings that are made from producing live theater is incredible, and we had no idea, so anybody entering in to this business without the idea that they are actually a pre-professional or will be coming in, should know this is a career path – it's not something to just dabble in. We need to start talking about how to make our lives better; how to make money to thrive. Everybody above us does.

In getting together and bringing all these people together, we need to start talking more about how to make our lives a better place for everyone involved, to make sure that we're taking care of ourselves. And that was pretty much the goal of just getting through the pandemic, making sure that our workers remain safe and that our rents were somehow being paid. We went from being a business in the black to in the red, despite the fundraising and loans. Now we just try to be on the road to recovery as a whole, instead of it being just me trying to figure it out alone.

One of the cool things we did to raise money was mount the "Showstoppers Exhibit" in Times Square which also raised awareness.

Brian Blythe: The Coalition is now trying to educate. One of the conversations that has come out in the pandemic is trying to figure out how to monetize design changes. So that as a shop we aren't eating the costs. There is an organic process that's happening during the design process. The Costume Industry Coalition is talking with Broadway General Managers because there are many shops investing a lot of time, energy, research, and skill into getting costumes onstage and by the end of the first build it's not like we are rolling in dough. Oftentimes those first builds can come in at a loss. This was a surprise to some of the general managers. As an industry we have to be better at educating people about the industry, which the shops in New York are trying to do. Educating stakeholders is important so they have a greater understanding of why it costs so much to make couture garments that are going to be danced in eight shows a week.

General managers are just that: they have a general understanding of what is happening in each area. It's important they understand, and depending on how the designer works: some designers are just the creative and don't get involved with their budgets so all of that is the associate. If you have a seasoned associate who understands the work they will campaign and work the budget asking for more money when necessary. Some of the younger associates are very timid. They don't want to lose their job and they want to be hired again so they want to make sure that these cost overruns don't reflect poorly on them. What we have had to say is this isn't a reflection of you, this is a reflection of the process, and if this is the process, there has to be money applied to it. Otherwise you're basically asking us to continually do more for less which impacts what we can pay our workers, which impacts us being able to survive to do the next show, so we can't be the ones constantly eating the losses.

I don't want to speak for female owners, but I do feel like an industry that is largely women and gay men, there's a sense of the feminized labor. Sewing is something you learned from your mom; it's not actually skilled labor. Which is so much different when people have actually trained or been doing the work for decades. They've learned so much over time that they can do this efficiently and effectively again and again.

This mentality of we all have to suffer for our art, and if we're not working really hard and many hours a day it's not worth it, that has got to stop. So please don't come into this industry thinking that that's acceptable, because it's really not. And it really should be enjoyable, it should be artistically fulfilling and creative, it should not be painful and grueling, and something that's going to just cause fatigue and burnout.

INDUSTRY PERSPECTIVE: AN INTERVIEW WITH SCENIC ARTIST RACHEL KEEBLER

Rachel Keebler has been a painter since high school and was a scenic art member of USA 829 from 1981–1994. Well known for co-founding Cobalt 1988, she has been Owner and Director of Studies at Cobalt Studios since 1993. She has been actively charging, painting, and overseeing the programs there ever since.

Rachel Keebler is a 1978 BFA graduate of Boston University where she studied scenic design and scenic art with Don Beaman and concurrently worked for and learned many of her painting skills from James Leonard Joy, an association which continues to this day. Having painted scenery in high school, Rachel began painting scenery professionally in 1977. In 1981, Rachel was accepted through the practical exam into USA 829 while she was teaching at UNCSA. Among other venues, she has taught at Temple University, the University of North Carolina School for the Arts, University of Michigan Kalamazoo, the Krannert Center, USITT national Conferences, USITT Chicago, USITT Chesapeake, and at the Hong Kong Academy of Performing Arts.

Can you describe your organization and your function in it?

I am one of the founders and currently am the Owner and Director of Cobalt Studios Inc. Cobalt was created to be an educational studio on the subject of Scenic Painting for the Entertainment Industry. It is designed to be a combination working scenic studio and teaching studio, in the grand tradition of Frank Lloyd Wright. I think of myself as the captain of the ship, the head chef, the coach, and cheerleader. That's my part in it, and I show up every day.

Can you describe a successful collaboration between your shop and the designer or producing organization, perhaps a collaboration that was ideal from your end? What makes a successful collaboration from your point of view?

I would say that a successful collaboration is characterized by everyone being happy in the end. I certainly could count on one hand the number of unsuccessful collaborations we've had over our 34 years. Success involves taking all the variables into account and the careful shepherding of the designer's desires through the whole process. Actually, it's the production that you're working for – so there are several people to coordinate with. We specialize in backdrops, and a lot of people don't think that backdrops have functions, except for just to hang there, but they often have other functions which need to be articulated in order to accomplish them correctly.

The collaboration starts with the producing organization and/or scenic designer reaching out to us to inquire and send us information. The initial information needed is when, what, how big, and how many. This information establishes if we could actually fit the job into our space and schedule. There is a guide on our website for how to initiate a job. Next the images are needed; also more specific information so that when I use our worksheet to figure out the bid I will be able to include everything we will be doing. Specific functions like if it's a translucency or a scrim, or if it wraps around something, or if and how it hangs… that sort of thing. For instance, in the case of *The Robber Bridegroom* for the Roundabout Theater; they employed us to do their show drop. It was to be a tawny color with the words *The Robber Bridegroom* on it. It was a large piece of soft monk's cloth that was hung in a draped fashion. To begin the show, they released it to drop to the floor and gathered it up "avista" and carried it offstage. So, learning the information about how it was going to be used was absolutely imperative; it caused us to dip it in a flexible ink which wouldn't come off on people's clothing or hands and stencil lettering in thin ink as well.

There are lots of other ways that backdrops are used, like going on tour – having to be made lightweight and portable or stand up to weather, or whatever. There can be many stipulations that go into these projects, so the collaboration continues with me asking lots of questions. I'm not in on the production meetings and I need to gather as much information about the pieces as would affect what we would be doing.

That's how it starts, but then it's making the bid, getting the job and shepherding the project through, based on that information.

And do you typically collaborate directly with a set designer, or do you typically work with a production manager or technical director?

It has to be both – there's the visual side of things, and the functional side of things. The designer doesn't always articulate all those functional things, and the technical people don't necessarily know what visual intentions are needed. Usually the functional information is clarified first, and then we clarify the visual needs.

Say, for instance, drafts can tell you the size of the piece. Then the material it's going to be made out of is discussed and determined along with what it needs to do, and then you figure out how to put the visual "candy" on it.

As the captain or coach, do you communicate everything you find out from designer and technical director to members of your team? Can you tell us more about your team on the ground, and that kind of collaboration you have with those who are getting hands on to execute the idea?

I hope I don't waste time telling them about all the discussions, but certainly hope I tell them all they need to know. The more that people I've hired know about the intents and processes that we're going to be doing, the less I have to micro-manage, and that's very good. Generally, when we're going into a new process, which is either for a backdrop with special needs or maybe painting on or treating a new fabric, there will often be a testing step to research and develop those unique materials and techniques. New needs and products equal different techniques. We'll hold it up, look at it under light, mash it up and see if it stays together, or something like that. But once the technical problems have been set and solved, once testing has been done then I'll present it to the crew I'll say, "this is what the aim is, this is what the approach needs to be, and so we're doing X, Y and Z." The orchestration of those people then becomes my job – you go do this, you go do that, and "we're going to put all three of these pieces on the deck with the bottoms of them all lined up, so we can snap lines all across all of them," that sort of thing.

Organization has to be by the captain of the ship and information has to be disseminated, though a staff scenic artist will know things others don't. For instance – how we order and put down our backdrops here. When we order the backdrops to be sewn for us, we allow for shrinkage by ordering them five inches taller if they're 30 feet tall. What happens is – the Scenic Artists draw a rectangle on the deck and pull the backdrop from the box. And they'll say, "oh it's five inches too tall," and I'll say, "well it's supposed to be; that is for shrinkage." The people who have worked for you for a long time know that I will give them the information about how large the rectangle is supposed to be, and they will fit it into the right-sized rectangle automatically.

If it's a specific painting process, it will have been tested in advance on small flats that we use – 2' by 3' in size. When I have someone in mixing color they need the information about how we're going to use it, i.e.: if the paint is going to be sprayed, it needs to be of a certain thickness – what part of the project we're using it for will help determine how much they're going to mix and what qualities it needs to have. Also, exactly what product we use for our color or paint has already been decided, so there's a lot of information that needs to be put together in order to mix the paint we'll need.

How do you relay information back and forth with the rest of the external team?

With the production team, it's almost always emails to a computer at the studio. I don't receive emails on my phone; this is a line I've drawn for my own personal sanity. So, I arrive at work, check the emails, and see what's what then go on the deck. At the end of the day, I'm checking emails again.

More and more it's just simply texting. Pictures taken right at the moment, quick questions from the deck. It's nice to have emails and have things in writing for more official, lengthy discussions but with a text you have it in writing and you get the answer right away.

I'm working with a scenic designer on the show that we're doing right now who lives an hour and a half away. We have great collaboration when he visits us. It's face-to-face collaboration in which we're walking around pointing at things. I grill him about what he really wants and show him things we've done and he directs us how to improve them, which is really great. The nice thing about him not being in house (and only just visiting when needed), is that when he arrives, he has a fresh eye. He looks at something, and says, "Oh that's crooked, or oh can we have that part be larger/darker/textured?" When we are working before he arrives, the scenic artists are on task. They might be drawing something, which is the first step. I'll let them draw, and I will walk over occasionally with a fresh eye and say, "that looks good, but let's tweak this part" but I don't catch everything. He'll arrive and say, "well this foot is bigger than the other foot!" More eyes are always better.

A really big point that we might make here is this: the quality of the artwork that comes to us determines how much interaction we really need with a scenic designer.

People have asked me, especially when it first started, what I thought about getting computer renderings from a designer to paint from? I believe that scenic designers should use whatever medium they want. The better they are at using the tools of that medium, to get as close as they can to their desired art, the better it will be. However – when they send me something, I would be smart to first say, "is there anything about this image that you would like to have different?" That gives them a chance to look at their work with a fresh eye and ask for amendments. I assure them that we are their fastest photoshop.

Whatever tool a designer decides to use to make their renderings is fine by me. They will have a spectrum of abilities with any one tool. One *could* say it's really great to get a hand-painted rendering, but if the designer is not good at hand painting and is great at photoshop, they should do photoshop. Whatever they can use to get the closest to what they want is key, because otherwise I'm sitting here trying to guess.

In response to the question, "is there anything about this image that you would like to have different?" one might get any number of responses. Hopefully changes are not radical.

Communication truly is key. A scenic artist, when in doubt, could (and should be able to) make it look exactly like the rendering, but one might look at it and think "this isn't consistent with the rest of the images" or "they can't be serious," or one might decide "I'm going to ask the designer if they want a small dark line around this to articulate it better" or "I'm going to ask the designer if they want some sort of texture through the stencil instead of a flat paint." Scenic designers who collaborate with their scenic artists stand to have their work represented in its best form.

In our shop, we'll do a sample to show you and I'll put it across the room so that when you walk in the door you'll see it from far away at first glance. I'm pretty direct about my thoughts and suggestions, but ultimately you (the designer) will decide. As a contract shop, you don't want to have to do things two or three times, so it is best to find out from the get go what is wanted.

Can you tell us about how you handle revisions as a contract shop?

It depends, which is my favorite answer. It depends how big the revision is and what it will involve. Whether you say "it will cost more" or "I can't do it in the time allowed" or "No problem" it will influence your relationship with the designer and producer, your relationship with the shop, and your desire for future relationships with those folks. One needs to choose one's response with thought. Remember – a successful collaboration is characterized by everyone being happy in the end.

FIGURE 5.4 Rendering by Christopher McCollum for Ballet Idaho's, *The Nutcracker*.

FIGURE 5.5 *The Nutcracker*; Ballet Idaho, December 2019.
Set Design Christopher McCollum. Scene Paiting Cobalt Studios Inc.

6

Pivoting Teams

DEFINITION

When set and costume practitioners are working on a play, musical theatre production, or dance work, there is a narrative and/or theme to serve. The particulars of the words, rhythm of the music, and/or the nature of the choreography provide the givens for the set and costume practitioner to propose aesthetic decisions following careful analysis of the source material, rigorous research on the scenario being portrayed, and discussion with all creatives working to serve the crux of the performative work. The technicians are concerned with the scope and feasibility of these choices within the context of time, money and available resources. When theatre practitioners utilize their abilities to meet artistic objectives in new contexts, they change an aspect of their product to meet the demands of the new landscape. The pivoting team member will decipher the language of the new context, and will expand their hard skills in order to complete specific tasks within the new industry. This is possible as the act of making theatre trains individuals to ask questions and find solutions, no matter what the scenario. Set and costume practitioners consistently adjust to new team dynamics several times a year as creative teams are assigned to different works within the same season, and designers and technicians often work for many companies over the course of a career and often within the same year, as freelancing in theatre is normative. This develops the essential soft skills necessary to work fluidly in any arena driven by visual communication and in any location, real or imagined, where a message is being conveyed and an audience is there to receive it.

The scope of theatrical training typically teaches a process rooted in a collaborative team creating scenery, costumes, lighting, sound, and projection content for a play or musical for a live audience. The terminology rooted in theatre practice is clear; the roles are clear though team size may vary. Creative teams outside of this scope have equally clear terminology with roles that are either highly specific to a particular circumstance or creative objective, or exist within a much larger team structure, with both necessitating an understanding that goes well beyond the fields of theatrical design and technology. These additional fields may offer opportunities for traditionally trained scenic and costume designers and technicians to pivot skill sets and thrive in adjacent industries in media, art, corporate, fashion, television, film, and events. The form and function of these teams will vary based on the industry and project being created.

The most critical skill set when pivoting to a team outside of your training is the set of foundational soft skills for collaboration as defined in chapter 1: communication, respect, emotional intelligence, transparency, dependability, and critical thinking. Strong soft skills allow for ease in navigating new teams and environments. Questions are asked, knowledge is gained through listening, and relationships are built through key behaviors: respect, dependability, and transparency. As the pivoting team member, you could view yourself as an ambassador for the vital skill set and training you possess. As an ambassador who has gained access to an industry or project outside of theatre it is within your ability to showcase the value of theatrical training. To successfully do so, you must employ your collaborative skills, and commit to your own professional development. The technical skills you possess are important but not what builds relationships with a broad spectrum of stakeholders. The tools of our trade are ever-evolving, and being an active life-long learner will allow the theatre practitioner to create work in a wide breadth of outlets.

To aid understanding of the pivoting of skill sets and industries, we will illustrate two examples in each set and costume team who benefit from team members with theatrical skill pivoting to join teams outside of the standard theatrical structure. In doing so, this chapter includes terminology for some of the most common adjacent fields that theatre practitioners have pivoted into for decades, and aims to acknowledge recent trends for theatrical set and costume practitioners in hybrid and virtual spaces.

FORM AND FUNCTION

The set and costume practitioner gains employment in alternate venues by presenting their credentials in a way that makes clear they work inside and outside traditional theatre models. It is commonplace in this day and age to see a set or costume designer refer to themselves as a visual storyteller on a resume or on their web-based portfolio. Theatre technologists and artisans also carefully choose the language to describe what they do so that their scope of interest is apparent to perspective employers. When pivoting, set and costume teams may find themselves in client-based lines of work.

With online job searching platforms, career websites, and the ability to brand yourself on social media platforms, practitioners have wide nets to cast when seeking work across disciplines. To work in an adjacent field to theatre, you might start by identifying aspirant workplaces and use the internet to identify positions that are available within that workplace. Networking and referrals are tried and true, and often lead to pivotal opportunities. Directors and performers might find themselves applying their skills to the screen, and they may call on their former theatre collaborators for support. United Scenic Artists (USA) and the International Association for Theatrical and Stage Employees and Motion Picture Technicians, Artists and Allied Crafts of the US, Its Territories and Canada (IATSE) group together are accomplished set and costume designers and technicians for the stage and screen, and through this professional assembly practitioners can become aware of a wide spectrum of creative activity within their reach. Joining a union and/or being represented by an agency who matches production professionals with clients in need of design and fabrication services can prove to satellite a career.

If you want to build a portfolio of work that demonstrates an ability to work outside of traditional theatrical venues, answering a call for proposals for art events and festivals may allow you to take the reins of creative direction and showcase the skills of you and your regular set or costume team collaborators in gallery or outdoor space. In ideal circumstances, if you are accepted to show work, a stipend for materials and other resources is provided. Taking this a step forward, practitioners may seek grants to fund new work that utilize their hard skills towards artistic works other than theatre. When design and technology join forces to educate, entertain, or call to action, scenography becomes the focus of the presentation and this work is hard to define. Grants, identifiable at arts.gov or through the support of library research, online funding campaigns, and patronage services can sustain the creation of new work and can foster collaboration. Set and costume practitioners can be client focused, geared to solve a problem that is already articulated for them, or can thrive in models of collaborative art making. We will focus on the latter as we explore what it can mean for a set team to work in an alternative venue. We will then discuss a client-focused way of working as a costumer pivots in a commercial environment.

The area most out of reach, but most in need of set and costume design and technology expertise, is for-profit organizations producing corporate work. We can think of corporate work as anything from working for a large technology company to producing a product launch to a pop star's tour. What makes working in these arenas similar to each other but different from a theatrical production is the importance of the "client". Thus far, we have discussed collaborative teams as circular in nature and lacking hierarchy. In corporate work, within a monetized system, you cannot get beyond the hierarchical structure. It is important for pivoting practitioners to understand the stakeholder's position within that structure. Even when working one on one with a performer, if that performer is at a certain level within their industry, they themselves are the company, the draw for the audience, and the reason for the project in the first place. This gives those individuals power along with great responsibility to produce a successful product launch, concert, event, etc. Navigating client-based projects relies heavily on soft skills, while producing a successful design demands a high level of hard skills.

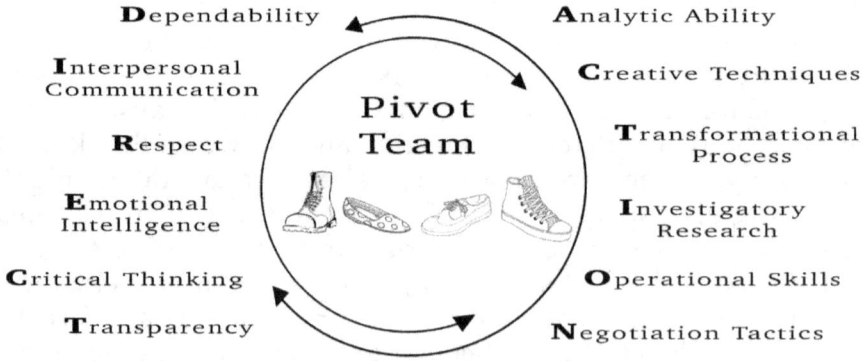

FIGURE 6.1 Pivot Team Shoes.

SET TEAM

Pivoting Industry – Performative Scenography

Form and unction
In this case a time-honored collaboration between makers is the foundation of creative activity in a new context, a festival or event that solicits works of art defined in a broad sense. Here the set designer and set technician collectively work as creative directors to implement their skill sets towards a different kind of artwork such as an automated sculpture, likely something akin to a fine art installation with significant fabrication or moving parts. The work is designed and engineered for a site which can range anywhere from formal gallery space, abandoned building, to outdoors. The outcome is similar to a realized set design as it is environmental, establishes a specific relationship between the art object and viewer, and speaks to a clearly defined objective.

Pre-production

When answering a call for work, criteria can be broad or narrow. The criteria can be digested like a script and director's vision. The set team then has freedom to interpret the criteria and has autonomy in establishing the focus of the work. In a field such as set design, where it is essential to take in the needs of many stakeholders (from producer to performer, from all creative team members) and reach a common ground so that all needs are met, it can be invigorating to step into a fine art realm where the set team can put forward their voice and vision without balancing the input from other creatives. The circle of collaboration exists within a narrower scope and firm outcomes can be established on quicker timetables. The outcomes are a direct result of a well written abstract. The designer might assume the role of "playwright" to write the abstract or it can be the result of a brainstorming between all members of the set team. Regardless, the abstract is what will have gotten you selection for inclusion in the first place, and will be a constant tool for assessment of the work as it develops.

If the work is destined for a formal gallery space, the building will have a manager of some sort that should be able to give you information similar to that of a tech packet for a theatre venue. The team needs to understand the physical space available for install as well as the size of entry points into the facility. Any technical considerations such as power availability and noise dampening, if relevant, can be discussed. Much like working in a flexible theatre, when work is at a site, the set team must understand the rules for public assembly including how to account for ADA regulations.

If the artwork is destined for a site not usually used for display, the set team's pre-production work is quite different as they first must scope the site and create the technical drawings for the venue. The technician on the team may find themselves explaining infrastructure such as power or rigging capabilities that are required for the work to someone who is outside of the arts but is responsible for the space being utilized.

The work of deciding what the art object will look like is no different than rendering and drafting scenic units for the stage. When envisioning the end product, the set team should be aware that their audience is beyond theatre practitioners so larger maquettes may be in order to get the idea approved in the first place or to further illustrate install needs to parties who manage the site.

Actualization

Since no theatre company is associated, you are left to identify shop space. It is not uncommon for set team members, both designers and technicians, to have essential tools for fabrication and finish in their personal inventories. The profile, and budget, of the art event will dictate if you are building in your garage or renting shop space. Build space is also dictated by the scale of what is being made and the materials and processes that will be used. Soft sculpted items will need much different space than metal work, and in all cases, whether it be fabrication or paint, the need to use materials safely is key and this too will dictate where you need to make the work. In functional teams there is the luxury of knowing where you will do the work. The major challenge on a fine art pivot team can be the fact that infrastructure needs to be put in place before work can begin.

The Run

Making sure appropriate time has been dedicated to load-in is key to the success of installation. The outcome is referred to as performative scenography as the design elements are the central character in what is viewed by spectators who can move about, and the technicians' engineering of these elements are on display. The work is generally viewed up close, and can have moving parts. The finish and the mechanisms of the constructed environment must be carefully crafted to communicate to the audience a sense of polish or roughness that is required. When the audience is welcomed to view the work, those that are left to handle the audience must have been given clear directives as to what is interactive and what must be hands off. These are new conversations as set teams don't need to explain this to well-oiled, theatre-making venues.

The security of the environment and the equipment being used needs to be addressed with fabrication. If the venue is outdoors many variables need to be addressed, rain, sun, and access all needs deep consideration.

When the exhibit is over, the pivot team must decide if storing the work is important. Will the work ever be installed again? Are there parts of the design or mechanism that can be repurposed in the future? Is hanging on to any sizable items worth the expense? The answers to these questions may be contractual.

Applying Skills – Set Practitioners in Film

The ability to draw, draft, fabricate, finish, and manage projects will open many doors for set design practitioners outside of theatre. Applying these skills to major film production can be freeing as your responsibility towards the whole can be extremely focused on one skill. In a theatre context, you might be the person deciding what everything looks like and creating all the supporting technical paperwork related to those decisions. In a film context, you might be expected to draft the footprint of a room for the art direction team, you might fabricate a single prop within a construction department, or you may be responsible for painting a single scenic unit. Although the set team members can grow into positions of more responsibility on film, theatre set team practitioners can get acclimated to new contexts by starting on the ground floor in positions they are well prepared to serve. The organization of the contributing designers and technicians in film, as well as production timelines, are quite different from that in theatre, but yet the soft and hard skills required are very much the same.

> **Activity**
>
> Take a scene from a well-known play and determine what essential requirements are required to stage the scene. Now imagine that scene is to take place in a usual context, for instance a department store or abandoned building. Everyone in the discussion group wears a set design hat. Together you determine a list of questions that you have for the producer. Then, write out a list of "must find outs" for the site visits. Reflect on these lists. What are the major positives for doing this particular creative work in this context? What are the major obstacles that must be overcome to make the project a success?

COSTUME TEAM

Pivoting Industry – The Commercial Stylist

Form and Function
The commercial stylist typically works as a me team or as a small self-managed team. In returning to the fundamentals of those two team types we understand that: the stylist will wear multiple hats thus fulfilling multiple roles with the pathway to the end result needing to be clearly and narrowly defined to the scope of one individual's workload. If there are technical collaborators in a self-managed team they will have a specific scope for their contribution to the project and are hired based on expertise and the needs of the project. For example, a commercial shoot might require a fantasy costume that must be designed and constructed.

We also understand that the commercial stylist is working in client-based design. This means clarity on stakeholder positioning is vital. For example, there is a difference between a styled shoot where the product is the star and a styled shoot where the individual is the star. Who is the client? A company? Or an individual? When working with the individual as the star or product, the complexity of navigating an image as well as the collaboration with that individual increases but shouldn't be thought of as a limitation of design but rather an opportunity to truly collaborate with a performer and contribute to their image.

Process

The process for a commercial stylist is short on time and the complexity of that parameter is often reflected in the simplicity of the styling. Styling implies working with existing materials to determine the way in which something appears. Stylists are wizards at sourcing: shopping is fundamental to the success of their work. As a theatrically trained costume designer, shopping is also fundamental to your training. The ability to source, understand sizing, and complete purchasing processes are common skill sets between costume designers and commercial stylists. The pivot that is required from traditional theatrical training is in the speed of the work and the ability to harness visual success through a camera's lens.

Key habits to develop in styling to accommodate tight time frames revolve around preparedness. When shopping, options in both style and sizing are important. Shopping for a closet of clothing and accessories to choose from with variety in both style and sizing will allow for flexibility during the prep and the shoot. The closet you collate is your only toolbox on the day of a shoot; how well it is thought out both in design and fit will have a great impact on your success as a stylist. A stylist's ability to shift on a moment's notice helps to achieve the best fit and look for each actor and promotes visual cohesion. Paying particular attention to the details that will be picked up by the camera lens brings authenticity to the story. As a character dresses for a scene they make choices in clothing and accessories that reflect the action of the scene just as in theatre. The key difference in wardrobe styling is the distance the viewer, in this case the camera, is from the character. Abandon ideas of stage distance and exaggeration as taught in theatrical costume design programs and focus instead on subtle impactful choices.

The timeline for work on a commercial and the amount of your time contracted can be as short as a period of 2–3 days. Upon contracting stylists are aware of general concepts for the commercial. Once casting information is available, a stylist will shop no more than a day to acquire a closet to style the shoot from. The day of shooting itself can be long with fittings marking the beginning of the day and final shots the end. Because this process is fast and lacks the depth of a traditional theatrical story, often the intensity of work that goes into theatrical crafts is skimmed down to necessity. Even on a custom garment, fitting and alterations time aren't available as in traditional theatre processes. Preparedness to adapt quickly and without much effort is essential to the successfully styled shoot. Multiple sizes and styles, construction techniques that allow for ease of movement, and adjustable items are recommended.

Understanding and creating habits around purchasing processes are a key skill for stylists and costume designers alike. Design work is not complete until returns have been processed but what does it take to get to that completion? It is extremely common and even recommended to have multiple sizes in a fitting: theatrical or commercial. It is important to understand and track vendor return policies in order to both accomplish work on this tight time frame and stay in budget. At the outset of purchasing, develop a digital tracking system for receipts. If shopping online, filing receipts with appropriate names in a project folder aids in the submission and return process. If shopping bricks and mortar stores, scan receipts immediately into a phone and follow the same guidelines: this will reduce the likelihood that a receipt will be lost. When purchasing multiple items from the same vendor, color code items to the receipt they belong to. The same color coding can be utilized to code items back to original packaging which will make returns processes much faster. Organizing items with purchase date and return by date on a spreadsheet also clarifies target dates in the event a shoot is postponed or more time is needed. It is the responsibility of the stylist to stay in budget and process all purchases and returns on time.

Applying Skills – Fabric in Design
Form and Function
Costume designers and technicians are well-versed in many skills. Chief among these is an innate understanding of creating detailed designs utilizing fabric. In recent years, spectacles such as touring circuses, opening ceremonies, and experiential installations have increased the integration of fabric-based elements because of the collapsibility of these elements. The expertise of trained costume designers and technicians when included in design and engineering teams working on scenic soft goods is clear. Complex patterning, sourcing of fabrics that are both visually complex and appropriate to the application, and finishing expertise gained through theatrical costume training are crucial to the success of teams creating elements

from custom curtains to inflatable scenery. Projects of this scale are completed by task teams. As a reminder, task teams are comprised of experts whose roles are clearly defined. As a costume professional you will pivot your expertise to a new type of project but you are the one expert on the task team who possesses your expertise.

Process

To pivot to a high-end scenic team as a costume practitioner means a pivoting of skills. The process will feel familiar to trained costume professionals as collaboration on theatrical work with scenic professionals should have resulted in a basic awareness of scenic processes. Fundamental differences in skill applications are easily navigated relying on principals of soft skills including effective communication. Shifts of scale, durability, and structural engineering are most notable. On a team working on a project of the scale to produce scenery of this nature, costume professionals can rely on scenic engineers, designers, and technicians melding their expertise in fabric-based applications with the extensive understanding of scale, durability, and structures that their scenic counterparts possess. Pivoting skills to new outlets and collaborating across expertise can have stunning visual results when the entire team understands their positioning on the team and the value of each collaborator. The work should be approached with openness and acknowledge that your communication may need to shift as your collaborators aren't steeped in the processes intrinsic to costume design and construction environments.

At the outset of the project, it is important as a pivoting team member you begin to understand the interconnected task team: who is responsible for what and how do these tasks relate? Workflow is typically a give and take or back and forth in the creation process so flexibility is key as is a baseline understanding of a proposed workflow. Your task team may be quite large and include non-theatrical members with specialized skills such as engineering or theatrical members whose task is very narrow but the impact of that task is vast such as an automation designer. A thorough understanding of who is on the team, how to communicate with those members, and what the priority is in terms of each department's contribution will aid in both team success and the success of a pivoting team member. Asking questions, opening dialogue, and active listening will be key habits to bring to this collaboration.

> **Costume Activity**
>
> **Costume designer:** Utilizing a given set of measurements but no photographs of a female presenting performer, please shop the following scene utilizing online resources that are readily available with delivery or pick-up times no later than three days.
>
> Brand: major brand appliances   Character/scene: mother at home with three children, early morning making breakfast
>
> **Costume technician:** You have been contracted by a scenic engineering firm to collaborate on the design and construction of a daisy that pops out of a deck and then collapses back into the deck. The entire daisy can be no larger than 2 feet by 6 inches when collapsed under the deck and no larger than 5 feet in diameter when expanded. Consider your materials and finishes:
>
> - What parts need to be structural? What materials might work?
> - What fabrics will comprise the non-structural pieces?
> - What are the steps to the process for construction from patterning to finishing?
> - Estimate labor time and costs.
> - Estimate materials costs.

CONCLUSION

The collaborative skill a theatrical designer or technician possesses lends itself well to pivoting. As practitioners the ability to utilize skill sets outside of traditional theatre spaces expands opportunities for employment and increases our bottom line while potentially offering creative fulfillment and expansion. Pivoting to join a team with similar creative goals but different systems for achieving those goals and different mediums of output can reinvigorate designers and technicians alike. Active participation in an array of teams strengthens skills and expands our scope and understanding of the collaborative, creative team. Systems in place in other industries can be useful to be exposed to and brought back to improve theatrical processes. Exposure as designers and technicians is key to continued creative growth. A commitment to life-long learning will open doors to new ways of creative expression and expand your personal tool set used to solve technical challenges. What better way to achieve that growth than to participate in creative projects outside of the norm?

> **Pivot Team Activity**
>
> This activity highlights the key differences to working in a pivot team: "adjacent" (discipline in theatre), "pivot" (other industry), and "alternate" (venue/physical space for making the work)
>
> In this game of "Adjacent, Pivot, Alternate," you will reflect on your last theatre project, and focus on the hat you wore for that production. Articulate in writing: what was your department, what were the three most critical hard skills to complete the tasks, and what three soft skills did you implement for success? Pass your answers to the left.
>
> Read the answers provided. Based on the responses, suggest an adjacent discipline the practitioner could work in (for instance, a set person might be able to work in a light department, etc.). Then imagine what other industries that skill set could contribute to. Finally, referring to the initial answers, imagine an alternative environment for which the work could have been produced.
>
> Repeat the pass to the left and obtain another set of answers.
>
> Pass the response sheet to its rightful owner. The practitioner, themselves, will report the findings and comment on what skills would need to be acquired to work in the adjacent fields suggested. They will also comment on the challenges that might present in the alternate venues proposed.
>
> This should be an open discussion where all participants can chime in and offer thoughts stemming from individual experiences. This is an opportunity to learn from fellow practitioners and a seasoned facilitator's experiences. This activity could also be purely self-reflective and used as a way to tap into one's own sense of self and what is possible in their career.

INDUSTRY PERSPECTIVE: AN INTERVIEW WITH DESIGNER CHRIS ASH

The hard and soft skills required for the design and actualization of sets and costumes for theatre can be implemented in the creation of a wide range of live and recorded performative works, leading to careers inside and outside the performing arts in arenas where visual storytelling is integral.

Christopher Ash (he/him) is an international designer and filmmaker that draws on 25 years of experience. His work has been seen in 16 countries, and recognized for 16 awards. Broadway credits include *Sunday in the Park with George, Saint Joan, Network, The Prince of Broadway, The Crucible, An Act of God,* and *On the Town*. His opera designs have been seen at Opéra national de Paris, The Metropolitan, Lyric Opera of Chicago, Canadian Opera, and Houston Grand Opera. Christopher holds an MFA in design from the Yale School of Drama.

Where has your foundation in set design and production taken you that you had not expected?

My start in set design is a bit ambiguous as I feel like I sort of started in everything, at the same time. But in branching out it allowed me to, on a very practical level, be more attractive to certain clients, or certain collaborators, because they know that I'm going to think about something from multiple points of view because I've been multi-headed from the beginning. Where it has allowed me to branch to most directly is in projection design, being a scenic designer and then collaborating with other lighting designers.

To what venues and in what role(s)?

My first projection design was while working on a ballet as the scenic designer, this must have been in the early 2000s. In this design I wanted to be able to change location. Normally we would have just rented backdrops and have something like 10 backdrops. We didn't really want to do that, we didn't want to consume all those linesets and ultimately change the size of the space. So I asked, "Why don't we use projections?" and back then it wasn't very common to use projections and everyone was like "Oh, what is that magic voodoo?" Ultimately the design we created was so successful this company has continued to use projections for all of their ballets.

One reason projection made sense for us was that I was really good at making images and using photoshop. I knew that was the kind of storytelling that we needed but, for me it was no difference between making projected images and making a backdrop that we would have painted otherwise. Except now we can have a sequence where you are able to melt the snow and create spring simply by cross fading a series of images. This is the moment I began identifying as a projection designer.

Can you tell us what theatrical skill set best served the new working condition?

As a set designer you need to know how to draw, and you should know how to paint. I knew how to watercolor and draw, and I had been making painted plates for backdrops for a while, so it really wasn't that far-fetched for me to create a series of images that were by created by hand using digital images.

Were there any additional hard skills that you needed to acquire in order to succeed in the new context?

The new skill I needed to learn was content delivery and time management when making content. I didn't realize how long it would take to "render" a moving image. That was a hard lesson to learn. Also learning how to efficiently deliver media to a media server like catalyst, and later Isadora became another skill. Knowing what formats, and codecs to use. How to make something play back smoothly when crossfading. What to do and what not to do to an image through the media server. It was all a big learning process with many mistakes made along the way.

I knew how to manipulate images. You need to know how to use photoshop. You need to know how to move and change and crossfade and animate things at a basic level. Lately my set design work has been directly affecting my projection design work as I learn how to create an entirely 3D process for set design and that skill is being integrated in projection design. We are now in a world where we can create a digital 3D environment that matches the live environment and then create mapped lighting effects. This is a skill I am continually developing. I keep telling students that as a set designer you should be developing 3D modeling skills. This is where these fields are going and will be skills that you're going to be able to apply across disciplines.

Let's go back to the idea of pivoting skills into new contexts and discuss your relationship to venue and how that has changed. Where do you work?

I don't have a typical type of venue or theatre that I work at. Which means that I primarily think about the story that's being told, and how I would like the storytellers to relate to the audience. Are we sharing space or is the space being presented to the audience? I'm always thinking about how I can play with the relationship to the audience. Even in a traditional space, can I bring the audience closer, can I put them on the stage, can I break those boundaries of the formality of the architecture? Those are the things that are interesting to me.

One of the first times that I experienced something that was a non-traditional form of "theatre" was in the late 90s in Buffalo working with John Rickus and Carlie Todoro-Rickus. We were doing this really crazy like rave art installation in a parking garage. I remember that being the first time I realized what we're doing is all of the same things we would do in theatre with the variation of we now need to have it accessible from all sides, we now need to have it approachable from any point of view, and the exciting thing is that it changes the background. This opened up a new way of thinking about form.

I have been working a lot as a filmmaker lately. It's all the same skills, you know, maybe a little less fantastic. You tend to lean into actual spaces and actual objects. But you're still asking the same questions about character and story and I'm trying to set up a world where the viewer, the camera in this instance, is getting information along the way.

At the moment I'm working on a ballet and an opera. I'm collaborating with someone about a museum installation. I am working on a series of short little films that are being released as what they're calling a CSA. I'm working on a series of longer films that will be released at some point on their own, but are also being integrated into a live show. I'm working on a cruise ship, and a historical drama. So I have a wide variety of projects and disciplines.

Thinking back on your formal training in theatre production, what are your views on the most viable areas to transfer those skills into, and/or what new opportunities do you see on the horizon?

There was a set designer in Chicago that I assisted early on, Jeff Bauer, who is also an architect, and he would do a lot of interior remodeling. Even though I typically assisted him on set design, I would often get my paid $20 an hour to help him do layouts and go in and measure apartments, create plans and visualizations. I think there's a direct translation of our skill set into those avenues where you can work as a draftsperson or work as an assistant in architecture, that kind of thing – very easily going into other commercial work, anything that tells a story you can translate your skills into.

I think the most important skill is to be able to be curious. Really dive into things that you're uncomfortable with and just be honest about your skill level and be willing to learn. Be willing to adapt to new circumstances. When I'm hiring people, I don't always hire the people with the most or the best skills. I often hire people with the best attitude and with the most interest in learning. There's one person who's working with me right now, who hasn't done any animation, but I know that they know music, I know that they have an interesting visual style and they're super curious. Within three weeks working in the studio around other more skilled artists they're making visually compelling material that actually excels at music and timing. I know that they have musical skills, I can tell that on every eight count they are making a new choice because they know that that's how music works and because of that they are able to make compelling choices. So, when you ask, "What else can I do?" I believe you can anything you want, so long as you're genuinely interested in it.

People who tend to find work easily are either very pointy people that are highly skilled in a narrow field or are very round people with lots of applicable skills to a lot of areas. The challenge with very pointy people, as we saw in the pandemic, a lot of those pointy people had a hard time coping with dramatic changes in the field. When there are no people to costume, or there are no environments to light then those skills aren't needed and many folks were left without work for many months. Whereas people who had a wide range of skills, anyone who had video skills, all of a sudden were given a lot of opportunities. Others were able to adapt and move into other parts of the industry. Many people didn't manage to adapt and have simply left theatre all together. You could see the people that had a little bit more roundedness faired a little bit better over the last couple years.

One of the most surprising developments of the past few years has been in extended and augmented reality worlds. It seems obvious to me that they need designers, that they need architects, that they need people who understand storytelling through images. They don't need gaming 3D modelers that don't know architecture; they need people who have a solid understanding of design and storytelling to be able to make compelling 3D worlds.

As you continue to broaden what you do as a visual storyteller, has your relationship to technology changed? How do you keep up with new technologies?

In school you spend seven years in a nice bubble with people helping you all along the way and then suddenly, you're in the world and you're on your own, without resources, and without guidance. There's no teacher, you're not being introduced to things. It's up to you to make the time to enrich your knowledge and skills along the way by going to conferences, finding opportunities to integrate new tools on a project, and by taking online classes or watching tutorials. Again, be curious, be willing to make the effort to learn.

Right now, I'm teaching myself Unreal Engine, and there's a lot of things that translate from one 3D environment to another environment, but this is a whole new environment – it's a gaming engine really. But now I'm starting to figure out how to harness this tool for projection and make content for the theatre.

And you go to that tool, because you had a specific problem, like a creative problem that you're trying to solve, and you needed something else? Is that how you arrive at the new technology that you would incorporate?

So, for this one project, we need to have a sequence where we're running through a forest. Simple enough, except forests are complex objects, so if you try to do it in Vectorworks you're going to be rendering these things for days, in order to do realistic lighting and all the details of the grass etc, not to mention that forests are evolving moving objects. Unreal engine has an incredible set of tools that you can literally just drag over a tree from their library into the 3D environment and it's beautiful. You have a variety of them available to use, you can populate a whole universe with them, and they are all moving with the wind. You can create a quite compelling living forest in a matter of minutes that will render out an animation sequence in near real time. This is huge! In some other

3D programs, it might take 3–5 minutes to render out one frame of a sequence. So, learning new technology like Unreal Engine not only makes the work better, but it also saves me a lot of time in the long run.

Now everyone is using Unreal for augmented reality, and extended reality projects. I don't see a lot of difference in the process required to design an environment for a game like Assassin's Creed, to set design or production design. One of the last sets I created, I simply took a lot of objects from a lot of different game engines, and I put them into Vectorworks. Theatre has a long history of adopting technologies from other industries. Early on we adopted rigging from ships to make line-sets and in the 80s we adopted moving lights from rock and roll. We've adopted all these other technologies from different industries, I think we're more and more going to be adopting video game technology into our worlds.

When you put the set designer hat back on and you walk into a regional theatre model situation, are there things that you feel you bring into the room now that you have had this breadth of experience?

With my experience I'm able to read a room very quickly – like who's in charge, who's willing to help, who's not willing to help. Am I going to be able to get the quality of craft that we need in this room or are we going to need to go outside of the room and bring in people with more experience? Through experience it's easier for me to look at the needs of a show and ask a producer for adjustments to the planned staffing. For instance, you might really need two props people because of the range of props required, or perhaps you need three highly skilled painters because there's a lot of trompe l'oeil, whereas someone who has less experience might simply accept a situation where they have a single inexperienced painter and not be concerned if that person has the skills to make the art that is needed for the show. I've been on shows where someone just doesn't have the skills, and you end up needing to redo a whole lot of work, sometimes by yourself. It's very rare that people will admit their skill level or admit that they can't accomplish a task by themselves. I think sometimes it is up to us to advocate for the appropriate labor because we have the experience to know what is required to get a good result.

With experience you learn that every director is a little different. I've worked with directors that want to talk forever about the design, and I've worked with directors that only want to rehearse with the actors and don't give design much attention at all. Often young designers need a director to carry the design process for them and guide them through every decision. At some point you begin to understand that you are your own director first, you are your own dramaturg first, and you need to come in with complete ideas. Then allow the process of collaboration help further shape those ideas.

Another thing that becomes easier with experience is knowing when what you are trying to do isn't working. It's a scary feeling, and it's an embarrassing feeling, but if what we're doing is in service of a greater story, then that's the kind of bravery we hope we all have when we are too far down the wrong path. It takes a special kind of dedication to the story to admit when your ideas were wrong, and it takes even more dedication, time, and energy to be willing to make the corrections needed after starting down the wrong road.

To the point of pivoting; pivoting hasn't been very challenging for me because I know at my core that I'm a storyteller, and no matter what I am doing to help tell the story I know that I will be able to contribute things along the way that make those adventures interesting.

FIGURE 6.2 *Doña Perón*. Ballet Hispánico at The Mahalia Jackson Theatre in New Orleans, March 2022.

Lighting, Scenic, and Projection Design: Christopher Ash. Photo credit: Christopher Ash.

PIVOT TEAM INDUSTRY PERSPECTIVE: AN INTERVIEW WITH DESIGNER ADAM GIRARDET

Adam Girardet (he/him) is an Emmy-nominated costume designer based in Los Angeles working mostly in film and television. Before making the move to LA in 2015, Adam lived in NYC where he concentrated his costume work mostly on theatre, contributing to various Broadway and Off-Broadway productions, as well as film and commercial work. This broad range of experience has provided him with involvement in genres running the gamut from ancient period to fantasy, to futuristic sci-fi, and everything in between. His most recent credits include assistant designing *Angelyne* (Peacock/Universal Television Productions) and *Hollywood* (Netflix/Ryan Murphy Productions). Adam's approach to costume design is to be the first line in the defense of character. He firmly believes that an audience can take in more information through costume, before a character even utters a line, than through any other medium on screen or stage. Clothing is after all a universal experience for humans, and it speaks volumes to all of us. Through deep collaboration with the creative teams on projects he always seeks to find the best answer to the question of character, all while striving to keep the visuals dynamic, engaging and in full service to the story being told.

Where has your foundation in design for theatre production taken you that you had not expected?

A foundation in set design led to a career in costume design. As a college freshman I was interested in theatre and architecture, so I took an intro to theatre class as an elective. It was there where I was introduced to the concept of set design. I was like, "Oh my God, this is it, this combines all those things that I love; it combines theatre, architecture and design."

The way my school was set up, they offered a set design major and a costume design major on alternating years. My training just happened to align with the set design concentration. So, while I was aware and interested in costume design, it wasn't really until my senior year that I was able to take more intensive classes and I absolutely loved it. While it was fast and I didn't learn as much as I would have liked in an academic setting about costuming, I decided that I liked it enough and that I was going to pursue both set and costume disciplines in my professional career. Once I graduated, I committed to figuring it out, and moved to New York. I took positions on off-off-Broadway theatre productions and student films to gain experience.

The truly unexpected place that I went to beyond that, is the career in film and television. When I was receiving my education, I thought theatre was the be all and end all and where I would be for my career. I ended up working on my first film set, a student film for my friend Anna. We've now been friends for 25 years and are still very close. I fell in love with the process of designing for film.

Can you tell us what theatrical skill set best served the new working conditions?

The education in set design gave me essential tools for costume design for theatre and film. I already understood basic design elements including color and shape, and was versed in the best research practices for narrative work.

What new hard skills did you need to acquire in order to succeed in the new context?

I was missing the very technical aspects of costume design. I taught myself to sew elaborate projects by taking apart old clothes and putting them back together. I committed to figuring all that out. And, as I did more of these projects, I realized that I was even more passionate about costume design than set production, so I decided to make that my focus.

When pivoting your skills to the new arena, what did you learn?

In pivoting from theatre to film I learned about the idea of continuity, and the huge part continuity plays in designing for film. I learned of the different working conditions, different stressors, and different work hours. The work style is fast, and it's like baptism by fire where they test you every step of the way. It's not to say that people are mean or evil, but they want to know what level you're at, and the stuff you know. You have to be sharp and always pay attention, trying to keep up while you pivot. Certain people on the team can be helpful resources to learning the lay of the land, especially on larger projects with bigger budgets. You have to find that friend, find that trusted person who can explain things to you. The people who hire you generally know what level you're at based on your resume and interview. I always felt comfortable asking questions of the person who hired me because they knew what level I was at.

In regard to job titles, responsibilities, and terminology, what differences were evident between theatre and film?

There's language in film that established practitioners deploy that can sometimes work to test the newbies. They'll say, can you hand me a C47 and by that they mean, literally, a clothes pin.

In regard to the landscape, what was learned about production timelines?

The most obvious difference between film and theatre is that in theatre, there is an opening night where everything needs to be done. In film, you have due dates every day. We design as the show's being shot. For example, I'm in pre-production for a 10-episode series, and we only received scripts for the first two episodes during this pre-production time. And even then, we only have casting of our leads, we don't have any background casting, and we don't have any information on day players. This leaves the costume team with a limited amount of work we can do for the series as a whole. And we'll be doing a large portion of the design work on the show as it is effectively being produced. In film, once you actually start shooting, it's go, go, go.

Staying ahead of the game and planning and time management are a huge part of design for film.

Like TV, it moves so much faster than theatre. That was a hard lesson to learn. In theatre, the design team is engaged much earlier than in TV/film.

Because of the rehearsal process that's necessary for a live production there's often more time to discover character, find out what's working and what isn't, and to actually bring it all together. TV/film productions generally have little to no rehearsal process. Things can change on a daily basis. The script that you get is often not the same thing you end up shooting. Couple that with common elements like casting not being finalized until days or sometimes even hours before the actors are on set, and it makes for a very fast-moving world where your production deadlines are much tighter than they often are in theatre.

I remember thinking how theatre production was very hectic, but the first time I worked on a film, I was like "Oh my God." The time allowed in theatre is almost luxurious, at least on Broadway. It's not like the smaller productions, and even the college productions that I worked on. On Broadway they'll sometimes start the costume process eight months before the show is due to have its first preview – roughly six to eight months is the norm.

The time of actually working under contract depends on the scope of the show. The head designer on a show often will have that show in their mind about a year or two ahead of time because these shows have a laboratory workshop/reading. In a lot of cases, a designer has already been approached because many directors tend to be tight with certain designers and production teams, and like to work with the same people because there's a familiar language.

In terms of when they get contracted, that's usually about a six month point that they are finally under contract and actively doing their research and gathering materials and starting builds, etc. The rest of the team usually comes on much later, about a month before production starts, which is when you start getting your supervisors. The dressers themselves, sometimes it's two weeks before and sometimes it's a month, it just depends on what the tech processes on a big show is.

When I was doing costume dressing work on Broadway, we started about three or four weeks before our first preview. And a lot of it is just prepping the theatre – the first week is getting the theatre set up, the second week just starting to get costumes on people and figure out rigging. A lot of times you don't have your first run through until that first audience preview. I remember working on a Broadway show where we did not get a run through until our first preview – there was no time to hang anything up, every costume for the entire show was just in a huge pile backstage. There had been no time to figure out when we were going to hang things up, and track them back to their racks, to learn that choreography – so that was a harrowing experience but we got through it.

In the TV/film world, the costume team is contracted with little advanced time. For the series I'm working on, I got a call on Friday, and I was working on Wednesday. We're about a month before we actually go to camera. The designer that I'm working with only started working the week before me. Four to five weeks of pre-production on a show of this nature, mostly contemporary, very little builds with mostly shopping, is pretty typical. On period shows that I've worked on, you get closer to 10 weeks of pre-production.

The pre-production process for the costume team depends on the needs of the department, but it's weeks versus months in terms of TV/film and theatre. TV/film is a much shorter process because so much of it is happening while you're actually filming that they're not going to give you six months to build the whole show when they haven't even written the script yet. In regards to the speed, I don't mind the sort of craziness of it, it gives me energy. It gets your blood flowing to look at that whiteboard with your dates, and be like, "well, we only have one week to get that done." It really lights a fire!

Good time management and also good decision-making is key – you have to be comfortable in your decisions, and you can't delay. That was actually something that happened on both of those live broadcast musicals because I think those designers were used to designing for theater. They would second guess their decisions and change because a lot of time in theatre, you have the luxury to do that. The ability to say "let's try this, let's see if this is working" and even in these live broadcasts, the rehearsal time and the tech time is more condensed than a typical theatre schedule. As the assistant designer, oftentimes my most important job is maintaining that timeline for the designer and I was having to really breathe down their neck and be like "we've got to make a final decision because this has to be locked in." There are no previews where you can keep changing it up until opening night, this is, the one night and a decision has to be made. It has to be locked in because these costumers who've never done quick changes before have to know what they're doing. Assisting was kind of like having to hold that hand, and be like, you got to make a decision today or it's going to be to the detriment of the production.

Regarding the design process in broadcast musicals, in both cases I was working with theatrical designers. In one case it was actually the person who designed the show on Broadway 20-some years ago. It was a huge leap from theatre to television for them and I was trying to bridge that gap. One of the reasons they actually sought me out was because I had experience in both theatre and film, and I had worked with them on a few shows on Broadway. They knew that I had transitioned into film and TV and so they sought me out to work here In La on the show because they thought I would be a good fit. Another challenge was that most of the crew out here had never done theatre or live productions. The"d never read a costume plot, or attempted a quick change in 15 seconds. They had never done anything like that, so it was educating an entire crew on how to pivot to this more theatrical style of producing a show. It was very different from what they were used to, and there were definitely some nerves. I said, "You're going to do this, and you're going to practice, practice, and practice." Those particular shows are set up a little bit more like theatre, and you do get to rehearse for at least a few days before you go live to air. You have to make sure your crew can get in there and get some muscle memory with what these quick changes are. Broadcast musicals were really a great amalgam of the two worlds – working on those was a lot of fun.

FIGURE 6.3 *Rent Live* – Valentina playing Angel Dumott Schunard Fox Television Productions, January 27, 2019.

Costume Design: Angela Wendt. Assistant Costume Design: Adam Girardet. Photo Credit: Adam Girardet

What was learned about TV/film industry norms?

Theatrical productions mostly take place in a linear fashion, at least pertaining to the story. In a film, an actor could be required to wear the same costume for months on end during shooting, and it goes through different stages of deterioration or aging. Film is rarely shot in order, so exhaustive documentation of continuity is absolutely invaluable to prevent errors.

In film you can let go of some of the constraints you have in theatrical design – a camera can be stopped, so you can make adjustments. You can even change an entire costume. I worked on a production where an actress had two similar dresses. One was built for standing and walking, and one was built to look better laying down in bed. It's that kind of stuff that you can get away with in film that you can't necessarily in theatre because the change has to happen in live time. In film you have more freedom to go wild with a design as you're not constrained by a physical change that has to happen in real time. Beyond that, I would say there's a lot of technical aspects.

There's the big stuff, like doing something with CGI work in post-production, and then the more tangible stuff like with fabric work. For example, if a fabric has tight stripes, it's probably going to "dance" or moiree on screen depending on what film stock you're shooting on or whether it's video, so there's a lot of technical aspects to that.

In film, have you found your work to be less collaborative and more in service to a client?

It is a sort of code switch from production to production. If you're designing something with a big star, they can become more of a client than the actual producers and it can be a real challenge. Sometimes in a fitting room you may have somebody who's very concerned about their image – and how that image translates to this period film that they're in or to a character that they're playing can be a puzzle to figure out. You have these challenges where a character who's supposed to be a blue-collar working-class guy with not a lot of money, is played by an actor who wants to wear $300 jeans. And you have to solve that issue and sometimes you win and sometimes you don't. Sometimes you can talk them into the discount store item that the character can afford and sometimes you can't. Depending on how important that's really going to be, sometimes you have to get your producers involved in it. You have this collaborative process where things are working great and then suddenly, they can be thrown right off the tracks when a person comes in and has very different ideas about what the character should be.

What's the approach you use when those deadlines are really, really tight?

Often film and TV in general tends to be more contemporary and not as "built" as theatre is. We're often able to shop off the rack which obviously allows for faster deadlines. But there are many occasions, like in a period piece, where that's not possible. If you don't have casting and you're two days out from shooting, the process is crazy. You go to a rental house and grab an entire rack of whatever fits the period, character and actor. You bring that rack to fit on the shooting day right in the trailer or on set. You have to prepare with a ton of options to be ready, and you also have to have an onset tailor ready to go for the little stuff, little alterations or anything that needs to happen. We try to be a little bit forceful about getting casting earlier when we know costuming is going to be a little more complicated. We really try to give deadlines to casting and be like, "You know we really need this person by this point or it's going to make life really difficult and it's going to make things expensive." Money talks and you know renting or building one costume is a lot cheaper than renting an entire rack or building multiples across a range of sizes. So we definitely use costs as a threat! We try to give those deadlines, and when they don't happen, you just have to scramble. One of the toughest things about film is that it's really hard to say "no, I can't do this, it can't be done in this time frame," because there are so many people who want the job and who will do it at any cost. Costume team members in film do get abused a little bit because of the nature of the work and people wanting to be in the industry. If you can't do it, there's someone who will.

We believe theatrical set and costume practitioners are well-positioned to contribute visual elements to all sorts of storytelling endeavors. What do you see as the most viable areas for this group to pivot their skills and succeed? Do you see new opportunities on the horizon?

It's an interesting question because it's evolving every day and really depends on an individual's idea of succeeding. There are many new opportunities being provided by web and social media productions for designers to leap on, but do those provide an actual living wage? I think one level of success is making a living wage and being able to survive on what you're doing. There are all types of media to design for, but you know they can be tricky to navigate if you're looking to make a living wage. There are TikTok stars, for example. The rare ones making millions of dollars can pay someone to design a proper production for them. I know people who have designed costumes for so-and-so's Halloween party because it was going to be on TikTok. They got paid well for styling that particular production. As you go lower and lower down the ladder these people are not going to have money to pay you, but you also do need the experience. We've all done the thing where we've worked for experience, and not pay, when trying to climb that ladder and get new opportunities. It's weird with young people, because the younger generation wants to get paid right away, but at the same time, do they have the experience to back it up? It's a great way to gain that experience, but not necessarily make a lot of money. Easy may be the wrong word, but I feel it's easy to take your theatrical foundation and pivot that into these new forms of media such as social media and web shows – you just have to make sure you can survive while doing it.

Can you share an anecdote from when you worked outside of the "four walls" for the first time, or perhaps from the most rewarding outside the "four walls" experience? What was your role and what was the project outcome?

I worked on a very small but ambitious little period-set student film. The director has, like I said before, become a very close friend, and we still work together now. She was attending film school and was being taught the proper process of filmmaking. The school did not have a costume design training program for films, so she was on her own. Unfortunately this is pretty common in film curriculums and costuming is not always held in the utmost importance. But that's a whole other discussion… Anyway, she asked me to help her out, knowing that I had experience. I actually did both the production and costume design on this film. It was set in 1957 and the setting was a schoolyard exterior, so there wasn't a whole lot of production design, it was just being careful of modern elements like air conditioners, stuff in windows and things of that nature. So the costume design really became the most important element in setting the scene. For the costume design, I had *very* little money and it was once again a little bit of a trial by fire. It was hitting up every Salvation Army and vintage store in Manhattan – finding pieces that would fit the period, or doing major alterations on stuff that didn't to make sure they were the right silhouette, all while working a day job as an office temp to actually pay my rent. But I had a great time and honestly, I would say that the little but ambitious film taking place in a period setting, with a small cast, was the perfect place to figure so much of that pivot from theatre to film. The period aspect allowed for a bit of the heightened theatricality that I was used to from designing for that world. But it also was really useful for learning what worked for film and what didn't. My first camera test for fabrics was a huge learning experience and also hilarious. They were shooting on film and did not have money to buy and process a lot of extra film. So the camera test had to be done in one quick shot, outdoors in a schoolyard on the Upper East Side with little to no equipment. Every piece of clothing and fabric I had acquired for this film – in one fell swoop. So it's me standing there in the school yard in the blazing sun making a rigid T position like Jesus on the cross with everything draped on my arms, on my body, or on my head. I think I had like four hats stacked on my head... But they were able to make sure these fabrics were the colors they wanted once they did the color timing process, and that they would behave as expected on film. That was my first camera test!

As things have gone more digital, it's a little bit less of a process than it used to be.Cinematographers and DPS can adjust a little more easily. It used to be white was almost a no go on film, especially in bright lighting. It would blow out the camera. But these days it's easier to make the adjustments to allow for it. You still usually want to tech it down a little bit, unless you want somebody to almost glow. In some cases we even still use a good old fashioned tea-dye bath. But for the most part, it's not the issue that it once was. There are bigger issues now. Green screen work has become incredibly commonplace in all levels of film and TV. Or if the character needs to be in green, then it will be blue screen work. Being careful that if anybody is in one of those colors, that it doesn't come too close to the key color. You can still get away with a lot of shades of green or blue, but you can't have it anywhere near that key.

And moireing – the "dancing" thing, that occurs with tight patterns like small stripes, tight plaids and houndstooths... We try to avoid stuff that's too tight, but if you really have to use it for some reason, then you do have to do a camera test and make sure it's not going to bounce around too much and start to move on its own.

How did the costume team make-up differ from what you have previously experienced in making theatre in traditional venues?

Even on well-resourced Broadway productions, it's usually a much smaller crew than on a film set. On a Broadway show you typically have your design team and supervisors. Then the actual wardrobe team dressing the actors. On Broadway they're referred to as dressers, as opposed to costumers on a film. That was a mistake I made the first time I was on a feature film set. I called the costumers dressers, and I was very quickly and firmly corrected… So anyway you have your design team, your supervisors, your dressers and, usually like a small maintenance crew that's in house stitchers and a laundry team, and that's pretty much it. On Broadway hair and makeup are not the purview of the costume department as they are in many other types of theatrical productions. Most actors do their own makeup on Broadway shows, unless it's actual prosthetic makeup. They're trained by the makeup designers who start the show and get everybody situated. The only time they really work together is if a costume becomes part of their design, as is sometimes the case with certain prosthetics.

Beyond that there are costume houses that specialize in catering to Broadway shows and designers. Most of the costumes are built off-site from the theatre. While hundreds of hours are put into the design and construction of these garments, they just arrive at the theatre, almost like magic, nearly ready to wear.

In film on the other hand there tends to be a larger crew and in many cases everyone is working in house. You have the design team – the designer and assistant designer. Responsibilities differ from region to region. For example in New York the assistant designer is expected to do the budget, whereas here in LA the supervisor does the budget. So then of course there is the Supervisor, followed by Key Costumers, specialty costumers, set costumers, background fitters and costumers, coordinators, shoppers, ager/dyers, costume department trainees, costume PAs, and costume transportation drivers.

When it comes to actual construction of costumes, it differs from show to show. Costumes can be built both in house by cutter/drapers on production staff, and they can be built by union costume houses with different specialties. If the needs of your show are fairly straightforward you tend to get by with one or two in house tailors or cutter drapers. As the needs start to grow so does your in house staff as well as the engagement of specialty costume houses. The average superhero or sci-fi productions will have an entire team of production cutter/drapers all while making use of multiple specialty shops.

My last show was not at all a huge production and we had 36 people on our crew, whereas I think the largest costume crew I worked with on a big Broadway mega-musical was around 25 not counting outside construction staff. This difference is required because of the pace required by film and TV. I know of film sets that have had 60 and 70 person crews when fully accounted for.

I feel like on Broadway because the crew is more structured it tends to be similar from show to show. It might differ in the number of staff depending on how large the show is, but I feel there's much less push back on the amount of crew than you get in film. Sometimes in film it can be very difficult to get the staff you really need to work at that pace – they don't want to hire an extra shopper, or they don't want to hire another customer – there can be a lot of pushback in terms of staffing. With production, it comes down to money.

Because theatre allows a little more time for collaboration during the conceptual and rehearsal process, you can really kind of figure out what's working and what's not. You have a little bit more of a sense of teamwork with those people, with the people who ultimately get to make the decision to say yes or no. You have more time to collaborate on that, figure it out and come to an agreement.

In film, there are times when we've gotten something ready and then showed it to the director or showrunner, and for whatever reason it doesn't align with their vision. Because there's not a lot of time to really discuss it you have to pivot quickly. You can make an argument for the existing work or give them what they want or need. If you feel strongly about something most of the time they will listen. It is still an extremely collaborative medium. It's just that the collaborative process is so much faster. So you often have to make that decision – do I take the time to fight, or do I pivot and go with what they're asking for and make it work? You can't sleep on it.

How did the costume team members communicate? When there are so many people on the team, how do you keep everyone on the same page?

My big question regarding that is, how did they do all this before cell phones!? It probably was actually pretty great because they had no choice but to slow down...

Constant and unyielding communication is key. For example, we will often have people doing background pre-fittings, especially if you're doing a period piece. You often need to fit your background ahead of time, and that can be hundreds of people for one scene. On my last show we did a scene on the Queen Mary, the historical ship docked in Long Beach, that took place in 1959. I think we had around 200 background fittings that were all done ahead of time. Because of the number of people and costumes needed, the fittings had to be done offsite, not in the office we were working in. And these are all happening while the designer and I are doing all the usual work of costuming principals and featured cast and prepping for other upcoming work. So we're not really able to be an active part of it. So these background costumers fit dozens of people every day and at the end of each day they put together digital boards of everybody they fit. They typically give around three or four options for each person they fit, and the designer or myself is able to go through and pick which one we like best for each person. We may not see these costumers in person for days or weeks at a time. It's all done remotely.

What were they given as a guide to kind of understand what they were trying to achieve?

They are given a lot of research – we print out research bibles. As an assistant designer, sometimes I'm the one doing the research. Sometimes the designer does it themselves. Sometimes, one of the costumers who's going to be doing the background fittings provides research that gets approved by the designer.

There's usually a visual – literally hanging the research on the walls of the fitting rooms, so that they can access it easily, and it is also nice for the actors. It gives off the vibe of what you're trying to achieve and helps them understand the design. The research is done ahead of time, and then given to those costumers as a guide to where they're going. And oftentimes the costumers that are doing the background fittings are also the ones responsible for pulling and sourcing the actual costumes, whether it be from rental houses or shopping or whatnot, they're often responsible for getting those clothes.

The design team has to go and approve everything that's been pulled and remove anything that they don't think is going to be right for the scene, and whittle things down, as well as provide clear notes on what is missing or is still needed. It's all a massive amount of preparation then followed by another massive amount of communication.

What was your relationship to technology in this new arena?

In film you're more constrained by the technical aspects. Will there be a green screen? Will this fabric work on film? CGI is a big thing you have to know – how to build a costume that the actor can actually wear, but then they're going to do something like add digital wings on it...

I would say on any TV or film set, the elephant in the room when it comes to the necessities of the design, is the camera itself. Once you know what the needs are, it often dictates what your needs are and what you're able to do. Everything you do has to work for the camera. The more design centric elements like what's the appropriate amount of detail, historical accuracy, and how the designs represent the character in both a wide shot and a close up have to be taken into consideration. And then there's the technical elements we already talked about – the fabric color. There's a process in film called color timing, where they'll completely change the overall look of a frame. They can make it look like a cloudy day, they can make it look very unsaturated, almost black and white, and if you need someone to pop in those scenes, you have to make sure that color is going to work.

How do you learn about what this cinematography team might be doing this time?

That's another important communication. We have production meetings where the entire production team will be in a giant zoom meeting. There'll be 60 or so of us. It's heads of departments and other staff and that's where you discuss all this stuff. You literally ask the cinematographer, "What's your plan for the look of the project? How are you going to manipulate what we're shooting? Is there going to be anything we need to know about?"

For the show that I've just started on, I watched the last season to prep for this season, and it's incredibly color-timed down to an almost black and white feel. I'm assuming on season two we're probably going with the same style since it's a direct continuation of last season. So we'll have to ask the cinematographer to set up camera tests with the wardrobe to make sure that we're getting what we need, they're getting what they need and we're all telling the right story.

And, then there's the classic comparison between camera and stage – in theatre you can have a big plastic zipper running up the back of a beautiful 18th century dress for a quick change and nobody is going to be the wiser. That obviously won't fly in film and TV – you got to have all those little buttons and hooks and eyes for when she turns to walk away in that close up.

After pivoting to alternative venues, when you return to the well-made play in a traditional theatre, have you applied processes or skills from the alternative venues to the making of this work? If so, can you walk us through how that worked?

I feel like the theatrical processes work more for film than vice versa. Film tends to be such a specific technical process that it can be difficult to apply other types of work. But on the opposite side it's very sort of accepting of other processes, because you can apply it to the behind-the-scenes work.

Is there anything I learned on film that I then applied to theatre? I have a really hard time distinguishing anything other than the fact that I carry my entire body of work and experience as a whole with me on every job I do, whether it's theatre or film, TV or commercial, or even a few photo shoots and styling gigs I've done.

The experience itself provides invaluable tools that apply to everything whether it's a film set or a theatre set. There are certainly things I've learned on film sets about collaboration and how to deal with different personalities and working conditions that I've taken back to theatre.

Any final thoughts on teamwork?

It was satisfying to work on those live musical broadcasts. I had people coming to me every couple of minutes with real needs about how to solve an issue that they hadn't really had to deal with before because this was for a live production versus a film production. That was a really cool experience because I definitely felt like an important bridge for all those guys – I really felt like I was firing on all cylinders. I gave them this 20-foot-long piece of paper that's all taped together, and they're like, "What is this?" and I'm like, "It's a costume plot. You're gonna love it, it's gonna be your best friend." For me bridging those two worlds was the pinnacle of teamwork.

7
Conclusion

Now that we have discussed what it takes to bring set and costume designs to fruition at a variety of scales and at different types of organizations, the underlying message is that the people skills, philosophies, and artistic and technical skills required for the making are relevant, regardless of the scope of the outcome. Personal attributes and a commitment to relationship building are what make teammates great collaborators, regardless of the production circumstances. Working to improve your soft skills, including being open to having your soft skills coached, will have a DIRECT impact on your ability to get and continue in set and costume positions, from getting your foot in the door, to maintaining connections with fellow creatives and organizations, to being asked back. In general, mindfulness of your own dependability, interpersonal communication abilities, respectfulness, emotions, critical thought, and transparency will lead to a healthier process from start to finish. Set and costume practitioners are not reinventing the wheel each time they start a new project, but they are imagining and creating unique designs for unique circumstances, so creative problem-solving on often tight timelines can lead to a fraught working environment. If one leads with soft skills over hard skills, a positive work environment will promote productivity.

Consider that no two shows or organizations are the same, so no two design processes can/should be identical, but they can all be built on the same foundation. Approaching show after show through a broken process results in grinding, unfulfilling, conflict laden processes and ultimately burnout. Working in a variety of team structures is par for the course – we've lived it. It is common for set and costume practitioners to find themselves on all of the team structures we have explored at one point or another during their careers: me team, self-managed team, functional team, and contract team; and for these practitioners to have found success and satisfaction in creative and technical fields outside the discipline of theatrical production. With each and every theatrical production or collaborative artistic project, the individual practitioner will be required to wear one or more hats. It should be a conscious choice how many hats one is willing to wear, with an eye towards how many hours there are in a day, and with an honest assessment of where their personal strengths lie. The smaller the team, the more hats an individual practitioner will wear. This necessitates depth and breadth within the hard skills categories, as more desperate specific hard skills will be called into ACTION for a solo practitioner, in service to the work. A single practitioner may need to analyze both the text and the technical minutia of the venue, create the conceptual drawing and fabricate the actual item, transform hard and soft materials alike, investigate the time period and research the capabilities of potential gear to be rented, operate a graphic design program as well as heavy stage machinery, and negotiate contracts and budgets for all phases of the production process.

Many theatre artists thrive on positive collaborations which keep our careers in live events. The adrenaline of a show and how the team solves the problem before the curtain is unmatched and how many "get the bug." However, a successful, sustainable career and life need to move beyond a continued mode of crisis. This is achieved by strong cohesive teams that communicate efficiently and respectfully. Every team member's contribution must be valued. Well defined systems and expectations aid production processes and keep conflict to a minimum.

If we return to the basic design process laid out in the introduction, and take into consideration the resources available in any situation, we can shift those fundamentals and define the collaborative process to better address priorities, make room for creativity, and fruitfully work to achieve our goals. Finding the right workflow, infrastructure, scale, and team will promote a thriving personal life outside of production careers.

The goals of collaborative theatrical teams can be defined as: successful storytelling, harmonious collaboration, and honoring each contributor's voice. To achieve these, we propose a different approach from the inception of each project that reflects that specific project. Harmonious collaboration and successful storytelling will result when resources are utilized respectfully and sustainably. The skills, both hard and soft, one implements as a theatre practitioner are directly relatable to other industries and often to day-to-day life in general. Respect, communication, emotional intelligence, transparency, dependability, and critical thinking are major tenets of soft skills which when recognized, exercised, and implemented foster all types of relationships.

Designers and technicians often enjoy a varied skill set and that can be the best part of the job. The ability to work on a team, regardless of size, shape or goal is the mark of a successful collaborator. Those who thrive in difficult production environments, especially if they push to fix them, will succeed wherever they go. Moving past a hierarchal team structure allows team members to be valued and do their best work for the team. Teams foster circular collaboration bringing givens and aesthetic solutions from the text through feasibility and into actualization and ultimately the show. The team needs to understand the value of each other.

The larger team, not referenced in the previous chapters, is the industry. As laid bare by the coronavirus pandemic, arts, entertainment, and culture is a substantial economic contributor within the United States' economy and has a worldwide impact. As practitioners, viewing ourselves as one team across the industry gives strength and voice to our talents, skills, and contributions. Making space for new artists, new ways of producing and thinking, and new voices allows us to learn from each other, creating an expansive industry. While we have proposed specific ideas for collaborative structures and skills, the inclusion of diverse viewpoints from across the spectrum of professionals offers the authors alongside the reader an opportunity for growth. We would like to thank our guests for their industry perspectives and highlight our takeaways from them:

Chris Ash: Take time to read the room. Be a life-long learner. We grow with each project in our ability to make visuals that enhance the story; as times change the tools will change, but our depth of experience as a storyteller grows.

Brian Blythe: This mentality of we all have to suffer for our art and if we're not working really hard and many hours a day it's not worth it; that has got to stop. So please don't come into this industry thinking that that's acceptable because it's not. And it really should be enjoyable – it should be artistically fulfilling and creative –

it should not be painful and grueling and something that's going to just cause fatigue and burnout.

Caitlin Cisek: Carve your space (literally), set-up your zone, set the tone for the professional exchange you will have with your collaborators; make it fun.

Adam Girardet: Learn to ask questions from your trusted source – the person who hired you. Be a translator for others, teach theatre skills to others – media production can benefit from tech theatre protocol.

Latiana "LT" Gourzong: Soft skills are both show-specific and organizational. A key to success in collaboration is putting timing on every decision.

Jian Jing: There is no boundary between hard and soft skills, they should be open to each other. When I draft, I consider it a love letter to the TD.

Rachel Keebler: Express the design idea in the best way you know. Throw out the idea that there is a best way or time-honored way, focus on the goal – clear visual communication.

John Kristiansen: Everybody has a valuable opinion and thought process. Everyone can make this a better process if we include the group into the conversation.

Brandee Matthies: Find the time that you are most productive and stick to it. Mornings work best – find the time to work without interruption.

Danielle Preston: When you are working with an experienced person, soak in what they do and how they do it.

Chelsea Warren: In a successful collaboration, you're all in a circle, holding space for the work in the middle.

Index

Note: **Bold** page numbers indicate tables, *italic* numbers indicate figures.

active listening/looking 4
actualization 14–16; contract teams 121–123; functional teams 95–97; me teams 35–36; performative scenography 148; self-managed teams 68–71
analytic ability 6–7, **24, 25, 26, 27, 28, 29**
Ash, Chris, industry perspective from 156–162, *162*, 180

bid process 120–121, 129–130
Blythe, Brian, industry perspective from 126–136, *128*, 180–181

casting choices 13
circumstance-driven priorities 13–14
Cisek, Caitlin, industry perspective from 47–53, *53*, 181
client-based work 145, 150
cloud collaboration 95
collaboration: actualization process 14–16; agreement on central ideas 47; analytic ability 6–7; bid process 120–121; cloud 95; contract teams 137–139; conversations 11; creative techniques 7; critical thinking 5–6; dependability 3–4; emotional intelligence 5; film industry 169–170; functional teams 81, 83–85, 93–95, 106–107; interpersonal communication 4; me teams 19, 20, 42–43, 47, 49; performative scenography 147; pivoting teams 169–170; pre-production 93–95; professional costume shops 117; revisions 132; run of the show 16; self-managed teams 56–58, 65–67; set teams 137–139; soft and hard skills 2–3; successful 41–42, 47, 107–108, 179–180; transparency 6
commercial stylists 150–152

communication: contract teams 122, 138–141; dependability and 3–4; functional teams 104–105; interpersonal 4; pivoting teams 174–176; self-managed teams 57; tactics 42, 48; visual/verbal 48
compensation levels, workload and 68
Computer Numeric Controlled (CNC) Routers 60–61, 105
computer skills 8
concept-driven priorities 14, 67
connotative research 8
contingency, revisions and 15–16
contracts, me teams and 22
contract teams: activities 115–116, 119, 125–126; actualization 121–123; bid process 120–121; collaboration 137–139; communication and management 122, 138–141; costume team 116–117, *118*; defined 1, 109–110; design teams 111; form and function 110–112; industry perspectives 126–141, *128, 141, 142*; maintenance and repair of scenery 124; monetization of design changes 135; pay rates 133–134; pre-production 119–121; previews 123; quality expectations 111; questions for technicians to ask 122; re-casting of performers 124; re-use of stock items 125; revisions 122–124, 141; run 123–125; set teams 112–113, *114*; shop structure 112; specialization 113; touring productions 124; unionized venues 123
corporate work 146
Costume Industry Coalition (CIC) 132–136
costume teams: activities 65, 92–93, 99–102, 154; bid process 129–130; Cisek, Caitlin, industry perspective from 47–53, *53*; collaboration with design team 131; commercial stylists 150–152; contract teams 116–117, *118*; crafts teams 90; designers 47–53; design teams 89–90; director/shop managers, connections with 90; draping

183

teams 90; dressers 92; fabric, designs using 152–154; fabrication meetings 130; film/theatre comparison 173–174; fitting process 130–131; functional teams 89–93, *91*; hair and makeup as parallel team 92; hard skills needed **27–28**; industry perspectives 126–136, *128*; me team 22, 24, **27–29**, 29–30, **30–31**, 32–33; monetization of design changes 135; pay rates 133–134; performers, interaction with 97; pivoting teams 150–154; pre-production 93–95; processes and outcomes by hat **30–31**; purchased items, potential of 64; re-casting of performers 124; re-use of stock items 125; revisions, collaboration and 132; self-managed teams 62, *63*, 64; start of projects 129; structure 127–128; wardrobe teams 90, 91, *91*, 92
craft, hard skills needed for **28**
crafts teams 90
creative techniques 7, **24**, **25**, **26**, **27**, **28**, **29**
critical thinking 5–6

denotative research 8
departments, hard skills needed in **24–29**
dependability 3–4
design packages 14
design teams: bid process 120–121; contract teams 111, 112–113
devised theatre 44–45
dissection of source material 12, 13
draping teams 90
dreaming phase 45
dressers 92
dress rehearsals, contract teams and 123

emotional intelligence 5
empathy 5
expectations of producing organizations 21
expenditure, tracking 70

fabric, designs using 152–154
feasibility: flowcharts *10*; negotiation tactics 9–10; revisions 15; team structures 10
film/TV: cinematography 176–177; collaboration in film 169–170; communication 174–176; costume teams 173–174; deadlines in 170; information provision 175–176; moving to 164–165; norms in 169; return to theatre from 177; set practitioners in 149; teams, film/theatre comparison 173–174; technology 176
form and function: commercial stylists 150; fabric, designs using 152–153; functional teams 82–85; me teams 19–22; performative scenography 147; pivoting teams 145–146, *146*; self-managed teams 55–58
functional teams: activities 88–89, 92–93, 99–102; actualization 95–97; collaboration 81, 83–85, 93–95, 106–107; communication 104–105; costume teams 89–93, *91*; defined 1, 81–82; form and function 82–85; hair and makeup teams 92; hard and soft skills 103–104; hiring staff 83; industry perspectives 102–108, *107*, *108*; information provision 84, 104–105; "jobbing out" 88; large 94–95; parallel processes 106; performers 97; pitfalls 84; pre-production 93–95; previews 98–99; production management 83; run 98–99; run crews 98; scale of production, specialization and 86; scaling 83; set design 86, 88; set teams *87*, 88–89; shop to theatre move 96–97; soft skills 94–95; specialization in 83–84; strike 99; summer festivals 83; technical rehearsals 97; technicians 85; workflow management 95–96

Girardet, Adam, industry perspective from 163–177, *168*, 181
Gourzong, Latiana "LT," industry perspective from 102–108, *107*, *108*, 181

hair and makeup: hard skills needed **28–29**; teams 92
hard skills: action 3; analytic ability 6–7, **24**; creative techniques 7, **24**, **25**, **26**, **27**, **28**, **29**; functional teams 103–104; investigatory research 8, **24**, **25**, **26**, **27**, **28**, **29**; me teams 22, **24–29**; negotiation **24**, **25**, **26**, **27**, **28**, **29**; negotiation tactics 9–10; operational skills 8–9, **24**, **25**, **26**, **27**, **28**, **29**; pivoting teams 164; self-managed teams 77–78; and soft skills, combination of 2–3; transformational processes 7–8, **24**, **25**, **26**, **27**, **28**, **29**
hardwood floor treatment, feasibility and 10, *10*
hat-wearing 3; contract teams 114, *118*; functional teams *87*, *91*; hard skills needed **24–29**; me teams 22, *23*; number of hats at one time 179; self-managed teams *59*, *63*, 66
hiring of staff 83
humor, use of 52

individual practitioners *see* me teams
industry perspectives: Ash, Chris 156–162, *162*, 180; Blythe, Brian 126–136, 180–181; Cisek, Caitlin 47–53, *53*, 181; contract teams 126–141, *128*, *141*, *142*; functional teams 102–108, *107*, *108*; Girardet, Adam 163–177, *168*, 181; Gourzong, Latiana "LT" 102–108, *107*, *108*, 181; Jung, Jian 102–108, *107*, *108*; Keebler, Rachel *141*, *142*, 181; Kristiansen, John 126–136, 181; Mathies, Brandee 74–80, 181; me teams 41–53, *46*, *53*; pivoting teams 156–177, *162*, *168*; Preston, Danielle 74–80, 181; self-managed teams 74–80, *77*; set teams 136–141, *141*, *142*; Warren, Chelsea 41–46, *46*, 181
information provision: functional teams 84, 104–106; pivoting teams 175–176
International Alliance of Theatrical Stage Employees (IATSE) 51, 84, 145
interpersonal communication 4
investigatory research 8, **24**, **25**, **26**, **27**, **28**, **29**

Index

"jobbing out" 88
John Kristiansen New York, Inc. (JKNY) 126–136, *128*
Jung, Jian, industry perspective from 102–108, *107*, *108*

Keebler, Rachel, industry perspective from 136–141, *141*, *142*, 181
Kristiansen, John, industry perspective from 126–136, *128*, 181

Limited Liability Corporation (LLC) 22, 111

makeup teams 92
Mathies, Brandee, industry perspective from 74–80, 181
mechanics of process 50–51
me teams: activities 38–41; actualization 35–36; collaboration 19, 20, 41–43, 47, 49; communication tactics 42, 48; contracts 22; costume activity 32–33; defined 1, 18–19; dreaming phase 45; essential tools 43–44, 49–50; expectations of producing organizations 21, 52; form and function 19–22; hard skills 22, **24–29**; hats 22, *23*; humor, use of 52; industry perspectives 41–53, *46*, *53*; motivation for 48; ownership of specific tasks 38; parallel processes 34; performers, relations with 53; planning 35–36; pre-production 33–35; problem-solving 20–21; relevance 18; research 40–41; resources 34–35, 39, 45–46; run 36–37; safety 36; scope, determining 40–41; set activity 31–32; set and costume teams 22, 24, **24–29**, 29–30, **30–31**; size of organizations 42–43; soft skills 24; solo practitioners in 20; strike 37; technical rehearsals 36; time management 51–52; types of performative work 44–45, 50; visual anchors 39; working spaces 35; working with other me teams 36; workload management 21–22

negotiation 9–10, **24, 25, 26, 27, 28, 29**

operational skills 8–9, **24, 25, 26, 27, 28, 29**

parallel processes, functional teams and 106
parameters, setting and communicating 68
pay rates 133–134
performative scenography 147–149
performers: as functional teams 97; re-casting 124; relations with, me teams and 53
pivoting teams: activity 150, 154; cinematography 176; client-based work 145, *146*, 150; collaboration in film 169–170, 174; commercial stylists 150–152; communication 174–176; corporate work 146; costume teams 150–154; deadlines in film/TV 170; defined 1, 143–144; example of 171–172; fabric, designs using 154–158; film production 149; finding work 145; form and function 145–146, *146*; hard skills 164; industry perspectives from 156–177, *162*, *168*; information provision 175–176; lessons learned from experience in 161–162; norms in TV/film industry 169; opportunities for 170–171; performative scenography 147–149; portfolio building 145–146; projection design 156–157; return to theatre from film/TV 177; set teams 147–150; soft skills 144; teams, film/theatre comparison 173–174; technology 160–161, 176; from theatre to film 164–165; timelines in film/TV 165–168; transfer of skills to other areas 158–160; venues and 158
planning, me teams and 35–36
point of view of a team 12–13
pre-production: collaboration 93–95; contract teams 119–121; costume teams 93–95; dissection of source material 12, 13; functional teams 93–95; me teams 33–35; performative scenography 147–148; point of view of a team 12–13; priorities, establishing 13–14; questions to ask 12; self-managed teams 65–67; set teams 93–95
Preston, Danielle, industry perspective from 74–80, 181
previews: contract teams 123; functional teams 98–99
priorities, establishing 13–14
problem-solving: critical thinking 5–6; me teams 20–21
process: activities 11; commercial stylists 151–152; fabric, designs using 153; *see also* actualization; pre-production; run
production challenges: feasibility 10, *10*; hardwood floor treatment 10
production reports 36–37
projection design 156–157
properties, hard skills needed for **26**

re-casting of performers 124
recruitment of staff 83
rehearsals: dress rehearsals, contract teams and 123; functional teams 97; me teams 36; revisions due to 15; technical 36, 97
requests for proposals (RFPs) 120
research, investigatory 8
resources: me teams 34–35, 39–40, 45–46; self-managed teams 56, 75–77
respect 4–5
revisions 15; contract teams 122–124, 141; costume teams 132; monetization of design changes 135; self-managed teams 70
rough order of magnitude (ROM) 120
run crews 98
run of the show: contract teams 123–125; functional teams 98–99; me teams 36–37; performative scenography 148–149; resources 71–72; self-managed teams 71–72; team dynamics and 16

safety, me teams and 36
scale of production, specialization and 86
scene design, hard skills needed **24**
scenery teams *see* set teams
scenic art, hard skills needed **25–26**
self-awareness 5
self-managed teams: activities 61–62, 73–74; actualization 68–71; budgets 69; collaboration 56–58, 65–67; communication 57; compensation levels, workload and 68; costume designers 62; costume teams 62, *63*, 64; defined 1, 54–55; different productions 64; form and function 55–58; hard and soft skills 77–78; hats, conversation about 66; industry perspectives 74–80, *77*; innovative tools, use of 60–61; limited run crews 70–71; Mathies, Brandee, industry perspective from 74–80; organizations engaging 55–56; parameters, setting and communicating 68; pre-production 66–67; Preston, Danielle, industry perspective from 74–80; resources 56, 69, 71–72, 75–77; revisions 70; run 71–72; set designers 58, 60; set teams *59*, 60–62; size of 58; strike 72; technicians on 60, 62–63; tech time 71; tracking of expenditure 70; variations in 57; volunteers, use of 68–69; workflow management 78–79; work processes 56
set teams: activities 31–32, 88–89, 99–102, 115–116, 150; collaboration 137–139; contract teams 112–113, *114*; design 41–46, *46*, 85, 86; functional teams 85–86, *87*, 88–89; hard skills **25**; industry perspective 136–141, *141, 142*; maintenance and repair 124; me teams 22, 24, **24–27,** 29–30, **30**, 31–32; performers, interaction with 97; pivoting teams 147–150; pre-production 93–95; processes and outcomes by hat **30**; reuse of stock items 125; self-managed teams 58, *59*, 60–62; self-managed teams, designers on 58–59; Warren, Chelsea, industry perspective from 41–46, *46*
size of organizations 42–43
skills *see* hard skills; soft skills
soft skills: critical thinking 5–6; dependability 3–4; direct 3; emotional intelligence 5; functional teams 94–95, 103–104; and hard skills, combination of 2–3; importance of 178; interpersonal communication 4; performers, interaction with 97; pivoting teams 144; respect 4–5; self-managed teams 77–78; transparency 6
solo practitioners *see* me teams
source material, dissection of 12, 13
specialization: contract teams 113; scale of production and 86

staff recruitment 83
stage operations, hard skills needed **26–27**
star dressers 92
story-driven priorities 13
strike: functional teams 99; me teams 37; performative scenography 149; self-managed teams 72
stylists, commercial 150–152

tailoring teams 90
team structures: feasibility 10; *see also* contract teams; functional teams; me teams; pivoting teams; self-managed teams
technical packets 14
technical rehearsals: functional teams 97; me teams 36
technicians: functional teams 85; questions from 122; on self-managed teams 60, 62–63
technology: Computer Numeric Controlled (CNC) Routers 60–61, 105; film/TV 176; pivoting teams 160–161, 176; skills with 8
tech time, self-managed teams and 71
three-piece suits, feasibility and 10, *10*
time management: me teams 51–52; timelines in film/TV 165–168
tools, skills in using 8–9
touring productions, contract teams and 124
tracking of expenditure 70
transformational processes 7–8, **24, 25, 26, 27, 28, 29**
transparency 6
TV/film *see* film/TV

United Scenic Artists, Local USA 829 (USA 829) 47, 75, 84, 136

verbal communication 4, 48
vision for a piece 12–13
visual anchors 39
visual communication 4, 7, 48
volunteers, use of 68–69

wardrobe, hard skills needed **29**
wardrobe teams 90, 92
Warren, Chelsea, industry perspective from 41–46, *46*, 181
wig designers 92
workload/flow management: functional teams 95–96; me teams 21–22; self-managed teams 78–79

For Product Safety Concerns and Information please contact our EU
representative GPSR@taylorandfrancis.com
Taylor & Francis Verlag GmbH, Kaufingerstraße 24, 80331 München, Germany

www.ingramcontent.com/pod-product-compliance
Lightning Source LLC
Chambersburg PA
CBHW070613300426
44113CB00010B/1507